HSC

FRIENDS
CliffsNotes
OF ACPL

The 1990s
Newbery Medal
Winners

By Suzanne F

IN THIS BOOK

- Learn about the Life and Background of the Authors
- Preview Brief Synopses to the novels
- Explore themes of the novels in Major Themes
- Examine in-depth analyses of the characters in About the Characters
- Acquire an understanding of the novels with Critical Essays
- Reinforce what you learn with Activities for the Readers
- Find additional information to further your study in Additional Resources and online at www.cliffsnotes.com

IDG
BOOKS
WORLDWIDE

IDG Books Worldwide, Inc.
An International Data Group Company
Foster City, CA • Chicago, IL • Indianapolis, IN • New York, NY

About the Author

Suzanne Pavlos received a B.A. in English and a Master's in Education from Stephen F. Austin State University in Texas, and a Master's in Social Work from the State University of New York at Albany. A former teacher of English and reading, she is currently completing a residency as a therapist.

Publisher's Acknowledgments
Editorial
Project Editor: Elizabeth Netedu Kuball
Acquisitions Editor: Gregory W. Tubach
Editorial Administrator: Michelle Hacker
Production
Indexer: York Production Services, Inc.
Proofreader: York Production Services, Inc.
IDG Books Indianapolis Production Department

CliffsNotes™ The 1990s Newbery Medal Winners

Published by
IDG Books Worldwide, Inc.
An International Data Group Company
919 E. Hillsdale Blvd.
Suite 400
Foster City, CA 94404
www.idgbooks.com (IDG Books Worldwide Web site)
www.cliffsnotes.com (CliffsNotes Web site)

Library of Congress Control Number: 00-105688

ISBN: 0-7645-8620-3

Printed in the United States of America

10 9 8 7 6 5 4 3 2 1

1V/RR/QX/QQ/IN

Distributed in the United States by IDG Books Worldwide, Inc.

Distributed by CDG Books Canada Inc. for Canada; by Transworld Publishers Limited in the United Kingdom; by IDG Norge Books for Norway; by IDG Sweden Books for Sweden; by IDG Books Australia Publishing Corporation Pty. Ltd. for Australia and New Zealand; by TransQuest Publishers Pte Ltd. for Singapore, Malaysia, Thailand, Indonesia, and Hong Kong; by Gotop Information Inc. for Taiwan; by ICG Muse, Inc. for Japan; by Intersoft for South Africa; by Eyrolles for France; by International Thomson Publishing for Germany, Austria and Switzerland; by Distribuidora Cuspide for Argentina; by LR International for Brazil; by Galileo Libros for Chile; by Ediciones ZETA S.C.R. Ltda. for Peru; by WS Computer Publishing Corporation, Inc., for the Philippines; by Contemporanea de Ediciones for Venezuela; by Express Computer Distributors for the Caribbean and West Indies; by Micronesia Media Distributor, Inc. for Micronesia; by Chips Computadoras S.A. de C.V. for Mexico; by Editorial Norma de Panama S.A. for Panama; by American Bookshops for Finland.

For general information on IDG Books Worldwide's books in the U.S., please call our Consumer Customer Service department at **800-762-2974**. For reseller information, including discounts and premium sales, please call our Reseller Customer Service department at **800-434-3422**.

For information on where to purchase IDG Books Worldwide's books outside the U.S., please contact our International Sales department at **317-596-5530** or fax **317-572-4002**.

For consumer information on foreign language translations, please contact our Customer Service department at **1-800-434-3422**, fax 317-572-4002, or e-mail rights@idgbooks.com.

For information on licensing foreign or domestic rights, please phone **+1-650-653-7098**.

For sales inquiries and special prices for bulk quantities, please contact our Order Services department at **800-434-3422** or write to the address above.

For information on using IDG Books Worldwide's books in the classroom or for ordering examination copies, please contact our Educational Sales department at **800-434-2086** or fax **317-572-4005**.

For press review copies, author interviews, or other publicity information, please contact our Public Relations department at **650-653-7000** or fax **650-653-7500**.

For authorization to photocopy items for corporate, personal, or educational use, please contact Copyright Clearance Center, 222 Rosewood Drive, Danvers, MA 01923, or fax **978-750-4470**.

 is a registered trademark under exclusive license to IDG Books Worldwide, Inc. from International Data Group, Inc.

Table of Contents

How to Use This Book

CliffsNotes The 1990s Newbery Medal Winners supplements the original works, giving you background information about the authors, brief synopses of the novel, graphical character maps, discussion of major themes, and a comprehensive index. A section of activities for readers reinforces learning with practice projects. For further information on the authors and their works, check out the section of additional resources at the end of the coverage of each novel.

CliffsNotes provides the following icons to highlight essential elements of particular interest:

Reveals the underlying themes in the work.

Helps you to more easily relate to or discover the depth of a character.

Uncovers elements such as setting, atmosphere, mystery, passion, violence, irony, symbolism, tragedy, foreshadowing, and satire.

Enables you to appreciate the nuances of words and phrases.

Don't Miss Our Web Site

Discover classic literature as well as modern-day treasures by visiting the Cliffs-Notes Web site at www.cliffsnotes.com. You can obtain a quick download of a CliffsNotes title, purchase a title in print form, browse our catalog, or view online samples.

You'll also find interactive tools that are fun and informative, links to interesting Web sites, *tips, articles,* and additional resources to help you, *not only for literature, but for test prep, finance, careers, computers, and Internet too.* See you at www.cliffsnotes.com!

INTRODUCTION TO THE NEWBERY MEDAL

About the Newbery Medal

In 1921, Frederic G. Melcher, coeditor of *Publishers Weekly* and founder of Children's Book Week, proposed an award for authors of distinguished American children's books to the American Library Association (ALA) meeting of the Children's Librarians' Section. The purpose of the award would be:

> To encourage original creative work in the field of books for children. To emphasize to the public that contributions to the literature for children deserve similar recognition to poetry, plays, or novels. To give those librarians, who make it their life work to serve children's reading interests, an opportunity to encourage good writing in this field.

Melcher suggested that the award be named after John Newbery, an eighteenth-century English writer, publisher, and bookseller who had a great influence on the development of children's literature in Great Britain as well as in the United States. The children's librarians accepted Melcher's proposal and, in 1922, it was approved by the ALA Executive Board, becoming the first children's book award in the world.

First awarded in 1922, the John Newbery Medal is a prestigious award given each year to the author of the book voted the most distinguished contribution to children's literature published in the United States during the previous year. The Association for Library Service to Children (ALSC) of the American Library Association appoints a 15-member Newbery Committee each year to select the winner of the John Newbery Medal. The winner is announced in January or February at the ALA's midwinter convention.

The Newbery Committee adheres to specific criteria when deciding on the Newbery Medal winner. The committee members consider the theme or concept of the book, plot development, character development, setting, appropriateness of the author's style, and the accuracy, clarity, and organization of the presentation of information to the reader. Because books contain different literary qualities, a book does not need to exhibit excellence in each of these areas; however, a book should have distinguished qualities in all areas that are relevant to a particular book. A book must also portray excellence of presentation for an audience of children. The Committee makes its decision based primarily on the text. If the overall design of a book, the illustrations, or other aspects of a book distract from the text, they are considered in the decision also. The Committee bases the award on literary quality and quality of presentation for children, not on popularity or didactic intent (the intent to convey educational or moral messages). The Committee requires that authors who win the Newbery Medal be citizens or residents of the United States.

The Newbery Medal, designed by René Paul Chambellan, is bronze, engraved with the winner's name and the date. The medal bears the inscription, "For the most distinguished contribution to American literature for children."

The first Newbery Medal was awarded in 1922 to Hendrik Willem van Loon, author of *The Story of Mankind.* Since that time, most authors have won the medal for writing distinguished fiction, although some authors of works of poetry and biographies have won, too. Along with the Newbery Medal, the ALSC also cites an unspecified number of "honor books," other books the Committee has reviewed and deemed excellent, and presents the authors with certificates.

The Newbery Medal is the most well-known children's book award in the United States. All of the Newbery Medal books and "honor" books are distinctive literature for children worthy of attention.

Introduction to the 1990s Newbery Medal Winners

During the 1990s, the economy in America was thriving, the stock market was on the rise, and consumerism was back with a vengeance. Technology affected, in one way or another, the lives of virtually every American. People used the computer to communicate with family and friends and to make purchases. The Internet became the fastest and most efficient means of obtaining information. American society was changing: Legislators began to pay attention to diverse groups of people such as the handicapped; environmental issues became popular concerns; and finally, the needs of children were beginning to be addressed.

The Newbery Medal winners of the 1990s are a reflection of the society in which they were written. Because people are using computers more, they tend to be more isolated from others than they were during previous decades. As a result, a recurring theme in the novels that won the Newbery Medal Award in the 1990s, regardless of the time period in which they were set, is the interdependence of people. In *Number the Stars* (1990), Ellen and her family would not have escaped communist Denmark without the help of Annemarie's family; Maniac, in *Maniac Magee* (1991), would not have a family if strangers had not taken him in; in *The Giver* (1994), Jonas realizes that people are not really living if they are not sharing their emotions, thoughts, and feelings with each other; Salamanca might not have come to terms with her mother's death if she had not had a good friend named Phoebe to mirror her own feelings in *Walk Two Moons* (1995); Beetle would not have survived long without the Midwife in *The Midwife's Apprentice* (1996); Nadia, Noah, Julian, and Ethan are connected as The Souls and as teammates for the Academic Bowl in *The View From Saturday* (1997); in *Out of the Dust* (1998), Billie Jo needs her father; and finally, in *Holes* (1999), Stanley and Zero must depend on each other to survive.

All the winners of the 1990s Newbery Medal have addressed issues related to diversity and the need that exists for acceptance of diverse populations—the experiences of Jews in a communist country, homelessness, prejudice that exists between blacks and whites, poverty, the elderly, adolescents who are considered outcasts or who are "different" from peers, and the handicapped. A common goal of these authors is to open the eyes of their readers to differences that exist throughout the human race and to suspend judgement until "they have walked two moons in another person's moccasins."

The environment plays a major role in novels such as *The Giver* (1993), *Walk Two Moons* (1994), *Out of the Dust* (1998), and *Holes* (1999). These novels portray the influence that a particular environment can have on people, their ability to persevere, and the appreciation for rain, trees, hills, or grass.

Because the needs of children began to be emphasized during the 1990s, it became clear that children's feelings related to grief as a result of death or some other loss were important to portray in order to "normalize" the feelings. 1990s Newbery Medal winners that included this theme are *Number the Stars* (1990), *Maniac Magee* (1991), *Missing May* (1993), *The Giver* (1994), *Walk Two Moons* (1995), and *Out of the Dust* (1998).

Other significant themes that appear as a common thread in the 1990s Newbery Medal winners are friendship and family, particularly nontraditional families, courage and bravery, and the dilemmas that adolescents encounter as they struggle to become adults.

All of the winners of the 1990s Newbery Medal are written for children in middle grade levels, and the protagonists are all around the age of twelve. *Out of the Dust* (1998), a novel that is written in free verse, is the only winner that is poetry. *The Giver* (1994) is the only winner that is written about a futuristic society.

The Newbery Medal winners of the 1990s are novels that portray a remarkable diversity, yet all speak to universal themes and subjects that are relevant to adolescents. The talents exhibited by the authors are truly outstanding and worthy of the prestigious Newbery Medal Award.

HOLES (1999)

Life and Background of the Author

Louis Sachar is the author of humorous and poignant stories for children and young adults. He published his first book, *Sideways Stories from Wayside School,* in 1978 and won the Newbery Medal in 1999 for his witty and suspenseful novel *Holes.* Sachar writes about topics familiar to children and young adults such as friendship, family relationships, overcoming obstacles, building character, and the consequences of choices. His protagonists are usually misfits—characters labeled *nerd, bully,* or *klutz* by classmates—who overcome their fears and anxieties while discovering their strengths through comical and realistic experiences and interactions with peers and adults. When Sachar writes, his goal is to make reading fun for his readers. Amidst the fun, he incorporates themes that encourage readers to think about right and wrong.

Sachar was born on March 20, 1954, in East Meadow, New York, to Robert J. Sachar, a salesman, and Ruth Raybin Sachar, a real estate broker. When he was nine years old, his family moved to Tustin, California. Sachar was a good student and liked school. He always enjoyed reading books, especially those by E.B. White. However, it wasn't until Sachar was in high school that he truly realized his love for reading.

After graduating from high school, Sachar enrolled in Antioch College in Ohio. Soon after classes began, his father died suddenly and Sachar returned to California to be with his mother. The following semester, rather than resume his studies in Ohio, Sachar enrolled in the University of California at Berkeley, where he majored in economics. Sachar's love of reading continued. His favorite authors included E.L. Doctorow, J.D. Salinger, Kurt Vonnegut, Kazuo Ishiguro, Flannery O'Connor, Rex Stout, and Katherine Paterson. He developed an interest in Russian literature (two of his favorite Russian authors are Tolstoy and Dostoevsky) but, after dropping a Russian language course in college, decided to take an education class because he thought it would be easy: All he was required to do to earn three credits was work as a teacher's aide at a local elementary school. The course involved no homework, and he was not required to write any papers. Working as a teacher's aide was a significant experience in Sachar's life, because it inspired him to write a children's book. At the time, writing was a hobby for Sachar; he never expected his work to be published.

After receiving a Bachelor of Arts degree from the University of California at Berkeley in 1976, Sachar moved to Norwalk, Connecticut, where he worked at a sweater warehouse during the day and began writing his first book at night. He was fired from the job almost a year later and decided to go to law school.

Sachar attended Hastings College of Law in San Francisco, California, and during his first week of law school, *Sideways Stories from Wayside School*, a book of short stories about kids who attended a thirty-story elementary school with one classroom on each floor, was accepted for publication. Sachar was unsure what he should do—be a lawyer or a writer. He did what most people would think the "sensible" thing and continued with his law degree, but Sachar continued to write children's books throughout law school. He graduated in 1980 with a law degree and passed the California Bar Exam, which allowed him to practice law in the state of California. He was not as excited about this accomplishment as his friends were; now he had no excuse for not getting a "real" job. Because Sachar's love was writing, he decided to continue writing children's books and to support himself by working part-time as a lawyer.

Soon after passing the California Bar Exam, Sachar met Carla Askew, an elementary school counselor (and Sachar's inspiration for the counselor in *There's a Boy in the Girls' Bathroom*). They lived together in a small one-bedroom apartment in San Francisco. Because they lived in such close quarters, and because Sachar needed to be alone when he was writing, Carla, who was very supportive of Sachar, would wake up early and leave the apartment, even when she was on vacation from school. Between 1981 and 1987, Sachar wrote *Johnny's in the Basement*, *Someday Angeline*, *Sixth Grade Secrets*, and *There's a Boy in the Girls' Bathroom*. He married Carla in 1985, and their daughter, Sherre, was born in 1987. Sachar's books were selling well; finally, in 1989, he was able to stop practicing law and become a full-time writer.

In 1991, Sachar and his family moved to Austin, Texas. He was proving to be a prolific writer of children's books. He'd had four more books published by then—*The Boy Who Lost His Face* (his daughter, who was one year old at the time, was Sachar's inspiration for the 1-year-old sister in the book), *Wayside School Is Falling Down*, *Sideways Arithmetic from Wayside School*, and *Dogs Don't Tell Jokes*. In 1992, Sachar began a series about the comical plights of an eight-year-old boy named Marvin Redpost, writing four Marvin Redpost books between 1992 and 1994, and three more in 1999 and 2000. After writing *Wayside School Gets a Little Stranger* in 1995, Sachar spent two years working on an adult novel. When the novel did not come together as he had planned, he quit working on it and began *Holes*, which was published in 1998 and won the 1999 Newbery Medal Award.

Sachar has received many prestigious awards and honors for his writing. In addition to winning the Newbery Medal Award, *Holes* was the winner of the National Book Award; a *New York Times Book Review* Notable Children's Book of the Year; a *New York Times* Outstanding Book of the Year; a *School Library Journal* Best Book of the Year; on the *Horn Book* Fanfare Honor List; a *Bulletin* Blue Ribbon Book; and a *Publishers Weekly* Best Book of the Year. Sachar has also received the Children's Choice Award from the International Reading Association and Children's Book Council, the 1987 Parents' Choice Award, and the 1990 Young Reader's Choice Award.

Sachar, Carla, Sherre, and their two dogs, Tippy and Lucky, continue to live in Austin, Texas. Sachar has an office over the garage of his house where he goes to write each weekday morning. No one is allowed in his office except Tippy and Lucky. After about two hours of writing, Tippy taps him with her paw or barks to remind him that it is time to quit writing because the dogs need a walk. Sachar has a strict rule that he adheres to when he is writing a book: He does not talk about it. Most of the time, his wife and daughter don't have any idea what he is doing in his office. Sometimes, Sachar spends an entire month just brainstorming. After he has written five or six drafts of a book, he lets Carla and Sherre read it, listening to their comments.

When Sachar is not writing, he loves to play bridge and tennis. He also enjoys other games, particularly video games, pinball, and basketball. Exercise is important to Sachar, but the oppressive heat in Texas has curtailed his outdoor running. (His dislike for the heat ignited his imagination and was the starting point for *Holes.*) Sachar continues to write fun books, hoping to increase his readers' ability to empathize with others and, as a result, become more caring people.

Sachar's Selected Works

Sideways Stories from Wayside School (1978)

Johnny's in the Basement (1981)

Someday Angeline (1983)

Sixth Grade Secrets (1987)

There's a Boy in the Girls' Bathroom (1987)

The Boy Who Lost His Face (1989)

Sideways Arithmetic from Wayside School (1989)

Wayside School is Falling Down (1989)

Dogs Don't Tell Jokes (1991)

Monkey Soup (1992)

Marvin Redpost: Kidnapped at Birth? (1992)

Marvin Redpost: Why Pick on Me? (1993)

Marvin Redpost: Is He a Girl? (1993)

Marvin Redpost: Alone in His Teacher's House (1994)

More Sideways Arithmetic from Wayside School (1994)

Wayside School Gets a Little Stranger (1995)

Holes (1998)

Marvin Redpost: Class President (1999)

Marvin Redpost: A Flying Birthday Cake (1999)

Marvin Redpost: Super Fast, Out of Control! (2000)

A Brief Synopsis

Literary Device

Sachar writes the humorous plot of *Holes* in a straightforward manner; however, he weaves into the plot three subplots. The subplots are tall-tale motifs that provide explanations about incidents involving previous Yelnats generations that significantly impact Stanley's life as well as the lives of others.

Character Insight

Stanley Yelnats (whose name is *palindromic*—which means that his last name is his first name spelled backward) is the *protagonist* (or main character) of the novel. An only child, Stanley lives with his mother and his father, who is an inventor. Stanley is a good-natured, kind, middle-school student who is ridiculed by classmates because he is overweight. Stanley's life changes dramatically after Derrick Dunne, a classmate who is much smaller than Stanley and is fond of picking on Stanley, takes Stanley's notebook and throws it in the toilet in the boys' restroom at school. Stanley misses his bus and has to walk home. While walking home, a pair of old sneakers "fell out of the sky" and hit him on the head. Excited because he thinks the sneakers will assist his father, who is trying to invent a use for old sneakers, Stanley runs toward home. The police stop Stanley and he is mistakenly arrested for stealing the sneakers.

Unfortunately, only Stanley's parents believe he is innocent. During the trial, Stanley discovers that the sneakers belonged to Clyde "Sweet Feet" Livingston, a famous professional baseball player who had donated his sneakers for an auction to help raise money for a homeless shelter for children. Stanley is unfairly sentenced by the judge and has a choice of going to jail or to Camp Green Lake. Because he is from a poor family and has never been to camp, he chooses Camp Green Lake.

Stanley believes that he has been unjustly accused of stealing the sneakers because of his "no-good-dirty-rotten-pig-stealing-great-great-grandfather." When Stanley's great-great-grandfather, Elya Yelnats (who never really stole a pig) was 15 years old and living in Latvia, he fell in love with a girl named Myra Menke and wanted to marry her. A pig farmer named Igor also wanted to marry Myra and offered Myra's father a pig for her hand in marriage. Because Elya had nothing to offer for Myra's hand in marriage, he went to visit an Egyptian woman named Madame Zeroni, who couldn't walk. She gave Elya a piglet and specific instructions to follow. If Elya didn't follow the instructions, Madame Zeroni would put a curse on him and all of his descendents. Elya had to take the piglet up the mountain to drink from a stream, and, while the piglet was drinking, he was to sing a lullaby. On the last day, he was to carry Madame Zeroni up the mountain, let her drink from the stream, and sing the lullaby to her. Elya did not take the pig up the mountain the last day, nor did he carry Madame Zeroni up the mountain. Instead, he left Latvia on a ship for the United States of America and from that day on, experienced bad luck as a result of Madame Zeroni's curse. From then on, the Yelnats family believed they were cursed with bad luck. Stanley was not really surprised when he was arrested; he believed it was just more bad luck.

Literary Device

Camp Green Lake is a juvenile correctional camp for boys. It is situated in the middle of a desert—there is no lake—and it is inhabited by yellow-spotted lizards. When he arrives at the camp, Stanley meets Mr. Sir, the guard, and is told that his punishment, which is the same for all the boys, is to dig a hole each day that is five feet deep and five feet in circumference. Mr. Sir tells him that digging the holes will build character and that he is not at a Girl Scout Camp. Mr. Sir also tells Stanley to give any objects that he finds while digging to Mr. Sir and, if the Warden (Ms. Walker) thinks it is worth anything, Stanley will get the day off.

Character
Insight

Stanley is assigned to Group D and given a cot to sleep on in a tent with the other boys in his group. He is issued two orange uniforms. His counselor is Mr. Pendanski (nicknamed "Mom"). The other boys in his tent are X-Ray (Rex), Squid (Alan), Magnet (José), Armpit (Theodore), Zigzag (Ricky), and Zero. Each day, the boys arise at 4:30 A.M. and are given a shovel with which to dig a hole. Stanley learns quickly that X-Ray is the unofficial group leader and that cooperating with X-Ray is essential to his survival. Stanley is nicknamed "Caveman" by the other boys and is accepted by them after he finds a gold tube with the inscription "KB," which he gives to X-Ray so that X-Ray can get a day off. After finding the gold tube, the digging escalates, at the Warden's command. Stanley realizes that they are not digging to build character; they are digging to find something buried in the dried up lakebed. Because the Warden believes that the gold tube was found in X-Ray's hole, she instructs the boys to dig in that area and not near Stanley's hole, where the gold tube was really found. Stanley realizes that the inscription on the gold tube could stand for "Kate Barlow."

Kissin' Kate Barlow was a feared outlaw of the Wild West. Stanley's great-grandfather, who had been riding a stagecoach from New York to California, was robbed by Kissin' Kate Barlow and was stranded in the desert for three weeks. He survived, claiming to have "found refuge on God's thumb."

Literary
Device

Kissin' Kate Barlow was the former Katherine Barlow, a school teacher known for her delicious jarred peaches. Legend has it that Katherine Barlow, a white woman, fell in love with Sam the Onion Man, a black man. Interracial relationships were illegal in the Green Lake community. The town's citizens set out to lynch Sam because he had broken the law and kissed a white woman. Sam's donkey, Mary Lou, was killed, and as Sam and Mary Lou tried to get away, Sam was also killed. From that time on, Katherine Barlow was known as Kissin' Kate Barlow. Eventually, Trout Walker (who had wanted to marry Katherine when she was a schoolteacher) and his wife (whose appearance closely resembles that of the Warden) find Kissin' Kate and intend to torture her unless or until she tells them where her treasure is located. Kissin' Kate is killed by a yellow-spotted lizard and indicates that the treasure is buried in the dried-up lake bed.

Because Stanley doesn't want his parents to know how miserable his situation is, he writes letters to them telling them about the activities he participates in at the "recreational" camp. Zero watches him write and reveals to Stanley that he cannot read or write. They agree that Stanley will teach Zero to read and Zero will dig half of Stanley's hole each day in return.

Jealous of Stanley resting while Zero digs half of his hole, Zigzag instigates a fight with Stanley. The Warden forbids any reading lessons and tells Stanley he has to dig his own hole. Zero is angry. He refuses to dig another hole and runs away.

A few days later, after a botched attempt to steal the water truck, Stanley runs away to rescue Zero. Stanley finds Zero under an old boat with the name "Mary Lou" on the side, eating jarred peaches that he calls "sploosh." The boys leave the shade of the boat to climb the mountain they see in the distance, the mountain that resembles a fist and a raised thumb. Because Zero is quite sick, Stanley carries him up the mountain. At the top of the mountain, Stanley sings the lullaby that has been in his family for years. The boys survive on water and wild onions. Zero tells Stanley his name is Hector Zeroni and that he is the one who stole Clyde Livingston's sneakers.

Feeling better, Stanley and Hector go back to Camp Green Lake. While everyone is sleeping, they dig in the hole where Stanley found the gold tube. There they unearth a suitcase. As they pull the suitcase out of the dirt, the Warden, Mr. Sir, and Mr. Pendanski are waiting for them. Stanley's lawyer and the Texas Attorney General show up. Stanley's crime has been investigated further by a patent attorney hired by Stanley's father. Derrick Dunne admitted that Stanley was getting his notebook out of the toilet at school at the very time that Clyde Livingston's sneakers were stolen. Stanley is innocent and can go home. The Warden tries to take the suitcase from Stanley and Zero, but the suitcase bears the name "Stanley Yelnats" on it, so Stanley can keep it. Because Zero's files cannot be found (they had been destroyed at the Warden's instructions, so that she would not have to explain why he was missing), Zero leaves with Stanley.

In the novel's last chapter, Sachar ties up the loose ends of the plot and the subplots. Stanley's father finds a cure for foot odor that smells like peaches and is called "Sploosh." Clyde Livingston does a commercial for "Sploosh." Hector (a descendant of Madame Zeroni) is at

Stanley's house with his mother. The Warden, Ms. Walker (a descendant of Trout Walker), is forced to sell her land, which is going to become a camp for Girl Scouts. In the end, the story's tone is one of contentment. Stanley has rescued Zero, and the Yelnats family is finally free of Madame Zeroni's curse.

Character Web

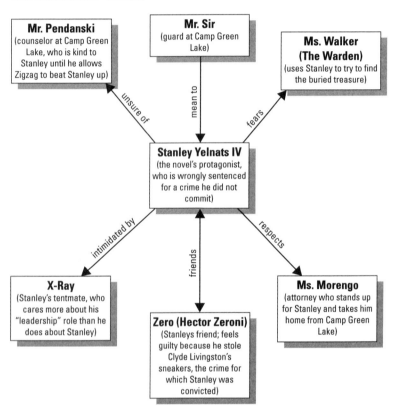

Mr. Pendanski
(counselor at Camp Green Lake, who is kind to Stanley until he allows Zigzag to beat Stanley up)

Mr. Sir
(guard at Camp Green Lake)

Ms. Walker (The Warden)
(uses Stanley to try to find the buried treasure)

unsure of

mean to

fears

Stanley Yelnats IV
(the novel's protagonist, who is wrongly sentenced for a crime he did not commit)

intimidated by

friends

respects

X-Ray
(Stanley's tentmate, who cares more about his "leadership" role than he does about Stanley)

Zero (Hector Zeroni)
(Stanleys friend; feels guilty because he stole Clyde Livingston's sneakers, the crime for which Stanley was convicted)

Ms. Morengo
(attorney who stands up for Stanley and takes him home from Camp Green Lake)

Major Themes

Theme

Major themes in *Holes* include the consequence of choices resulting from fate and destiny and the importance of friendship. Sachar never sets out to teach a specific moral or lesson when he writes. Instead, he creates characters that his readers can empathize with and involves them in plots that are fun to read. As a result, he believes his readers will naturally become better people.

Literary Device

Throughout the novel, fate, which is a power or force that is thought to decide future events, is a major theme. Stanley and his father have always had bad luck. They are sure their bad luck can be attributed to the curse that Madame Zeroni put on Stanley's great-great-grandfather and future generations of Yelnats after he broke his promise to her. Stanley and his father expect to have bad luck. When Clyde Livingston's sneakers "fell from the sky," Stanley was sure the sneakers were a "sign." He thought they were "like a gift from God" and might be the "key to his father's invention." Stanley believes he is "holding destiny's shoes."

Even though Stanley is arrested, the consequence of his choice to run home with the sneakers is determined by fate. Stanley is wrongly accused of stealing Clyde Livingston's sneakers and chooses to go to Camp Green Lake instead of jail. He finds a lipstick tube while digging his hole in the desert at Camp Green Lake and figures out that it belonged to Kissin' Kate Barlow, who just *happened* to have robbed his great-grandfather as he traveled West on a stagecoach with the fortune he'd made on the stock market. He was stranded in the Texas desert. Green Lake dried up and the community ceased to exist after a drought cursed Green Lake (Green Lake was cursed after Sam the Onion Man was killed and Katherine Barlow's school was destroyed). Stanley's great-grandfather survived finding "refuge on God's thumb." Nobody ever understood what he meant until Stanley sees a mountain in the distance while he is digging a hole, which resembles a fist and a thumb.

Stanley is later accused of taking Mr. Sir's sunflower seeds and ends up in the Warden's cabin. He gets her makeup case from another room, and, as fate would have it, it is just like his mother's. Unbeknownst to Stanley, the Warden bears a close resemblance to Trout Walker's wife. (Trout walker and his wife went to the cabin the Warden is living in, years ago, intending to torture Kissin' Kate Barlow—who was living in the cabin—until she told him where she'd buried her "treasure.")

It is fate that brings Stanley and Zero (whose name is Hector Zeroni) to the base of the mountain that looks like a fist and a thumb. Because Zero is too sick to climb the mountain, Stanley carries him to the top. Once there, Stanley finds water and sings the lullaby that had been in his family for several generations—the same lullaby that his great-great-grandfather was supposed to have sung to Madame Zeroni after carrying *her* to the top of the mountain in Latvia.

Stanley and Zero return to Camp Green Lake and find the buried "treasure"—an old suitcase—and again, fate steps in. The suitcase has the name "Stanley Yelnats" on it, so he gets to keep it, and the yellow-spotted lizards won't bite them because they have been eating onions and yellow-spotted lizards don't like "onion blood."

Fate intervenes when Stanley's lawyer, Ms. Morengo, arrives at Camp Green Lake at the perfect moment. Stanley is innocent and, because the Warden destroyed Zero's files, he can leave also. Stanley has reached his destiny. He fulfilled his great-great-grandfather's promise to Madame Zeroni and the family believes the curse has been lifted.

Theme

Friendship is another major theme in *Holes*. Before Stanley goes to Camp Green Lake, he doesn't have any friends. He is overweight and is larger than his classmates. As a consequence, he is picked on and teased. Stanley is a misfit and he knows it. Between his low self-esteem and bad luck, Stanley is quite unhappy. After being at Camp Green Lake for a few weeks, Stanley realizes he is larger than the boys in his tent, but he is no longer fat—the shoveling has strengthened his muscles. The boys respect his size and give him the nickname "Caveman." A bond develops between Stanley and the boys. He gives X-Ray the lipstick tube he finds and takes the blame for Magnet when he stole Mr. Sir's sunflower seeds. Stanley understands the hierarchy that exists amongst the boys; consequently, they learn to trust Stanley.

Character Insight

Stanley and Zero form a close friendship. Zero trusts Stanley enough to reveal that he can not read or write. Stanley doesn't laugh at him. Instead he begins to teach Zero how to read and realizes that Zero is quite intelligent. Zero fights for Stanley and after he runs away, Stanley worries about him until he realizes his only choice is to go find him. Stanley's yearning to rescue Zero empowers him to carry Zero up the side of the mountain. Sitting on top of the mountain, Stanley is happy. He likes the person he has become and he feels good because he has a friend.

Another theme that is evident in the novel is family relationships—Stanley has a loving family and Zero has no family. Racism is evident when Sam the Onion Man and Katherine Barlow are punished because they have an interracial relationship and when Zero is called Stanley's "slave" by the other boys when he digs half of Stanley's hole. The influence of the environment on the actions of people is evident when the extreme heat and lack of shade anywhere makes the boys' "blood boil." Finally, a theme that Sachar revisits in other books is evident. That theme is the compassion for society's underdogs. Stanley and Zero are misfits, but when given the opportunity to prove themselves, they exhibit their strengths and rise above the negative judgments others make about them.

About the Characters

Stanley Yelnats IV

Stanley, the protagonist of *Holes*, is a dynamic character. He changes during the course of the novel due to the influence and effect of his experiences and actions. As the novel begins, Stanley has low self-esteem. He is overweight and is accustomed to having bad luck. He attributes this bad luck to his "no-good-dirty-rotten-pig-stealing-great-great-grand-father," who caused Madame Zeroni to put a curse on the Yelnats family. Stanley has no friends. He is a misfit in his class at school. Because he is larger in size than his classmates, teachers wrongly assume he can take care of himself when he is being mistreated, so they don't intervene and Stanley is left to fend for himself. But Stanley is naive, innocent, and kindhearted, and he doesn't know how to be mean. He loves and respects his parents; in fact, he was trying to help his father by taking the smelly sneakers that had "fallen from the sky" home to him (his father was trying to invent a use for old sneakers).

Stanley is perceptive. When he arrives at Camp Green Lake, he quickly understands what he needs to do to survive. He follows the rules without question and he needs X-Ray, the unofficial leader of the boys, to think he is a good guy. Stanley wins X-Ray's approval by becoming enmeshed in the routine that is already established at Camp Green Lake. Stanley gives the gold lipstick tube to X-Ray to claim as his "find," and he takes the blame for stealing Mr. Sir's sunflower seeds, even though he didn't do it. Stanley is smart. He tells X-Ray how to get more time off and begins to teach Zero how to read. He perseveres. Hopeful and optimistic, Stanley keeps going despite the obstacles that he faces.

While he is at Camp Green Lake, Stanley changes. His body begins to change as a result of the shoveling, and he is no longer fat. Stanley's body is firm because his muscles have strengthened, and he realizes that he is the biggest boy in his tent. For the first time, Stanley is not ashamed to be the biggest. He is proud of himself and has gained self-confidence. Stanley makes friends and, when he is on the mountain with Zero, despite the ordeal he is going through, he likes himself and is happy. Stanley is a hero. He saves Zero's life, discovers the buried "treasure," and, because his plight draws attention to Camp Green Lake, the camp is closed down and no other boys will ever have to dig holes again. Stanley uses the money that he receives from the stocks that were in the suitcase to buy his parents a house and to build a laboratory in the basement for his father.

Zero (Hector Zeroni)

Zero is the novel's *deuteragonist*, the character second in importance. Zero's great-great-grandmother was Madame Zeroni, who put a curse on generations of the Yelnats family. Zero is dark-skinned and small in stature. He is quiet (in fact, he rarely speaks), and he doesn't readily reveal his thoughts, feelings, or emotions. A rare smile spreads across his entire face. Because he always hides what he's thinking and feeling, and because he keeps to himself, people assume Zero is stupid, but he isn't. He is quite intelligent and is particularly good in math. Zero watches Stanley write letters to his mother, and, finally, when he thinks he can trust Stanley, Zero admits that he can't read or write. He asks Stanley to teach him. Zero becomes frustrated when the Warden forbids Stanley to teach him, and Zero runs away. When Stanley finds Zero in the desert, they become loyal friends. Zero reveals that his name is Hector Zeroni, that he has been homeless for most of his life, and that he has no family. He is a "ward of the state." He told Stanley that his mother used to sing him a lullaby similar to the one Stanley knows, and he admits that he was the one who stole Clyde Livingston's sneakers. He was sent to Camp Green Lake because he'd stolen a pair of sneakers from a store the day after he'd taken Clyde Livingston's sneakers.

After finding the suitcase belonging to Stanley's great-grandfather, Zero used some of his money (which amounted to almost a million dollars) to hire private investigators to find his mother. The investigators succeed, and Zero and his mother are reunited.

Madame Zeroni

Madame Zeroni is an old Egyptian gypsy storyteller. She is dark-skinned and has a wide mouth. Because she has no left foot, she uses a wheelchair. She is a compassionate woman, and yet she is also realistic. Madame Zeroni wants to help Elya Yelnats when he tells her about wanting to marry Myra Menke; however, Madame Zeroni is direct with Elya. She tells him that the girl's head is empty, that she is foolish and spoiled. And then she spits on the dirt (the same way Zero spits in each hole after he finishes digging). She gives Elya a piglet and specific instructions about what he needs to do in order to ensure that the pig will be large enough to win Myra's hand in marriage. Because Elya does not follow her instructions, Madame Zeroni puts a curse on him and on future generations of Yelnats.

Elya Yelnats

Elya Yelnats is Stanley's "no-good-dirty-rotten-pig-stealing-great-great-grandfather" who is blamed for everything bad that happens to future generations of his family. Although he never actually steals a pig, his actions cause Madame Zeroni to put a curse on him and all his descendants.

When Elya is 15 years old, living in Latvia, he falls in love with Myra Menke and wants to marry her. Igor, a pig farmer, also wants to marry Myra and offers a pig for her hand in marriage. Not knowing what to do, Elya goes to see Madame Zeroni. Madame Zeroni gives Elya a piglet along with specific instructions. He is to take the pig up the mountain each day and sing a lullaby to the pig as it drinks from the stream. On the last day, he is to take the pig up the mountain before taking it to Myra's father and then carry Madame Zeroni up the mountain, too, singing the lullaby to her as she drinks from the stream.

Because he is vain and doesn't want to smell like a pig when he goes to Myra's house to try to win her hand in marriage, Elya doesn't take the pig up the mountain the last day, nor does he take Madame Zeroni up the mountain. When he realizes that Myra doesn't love him, Elya gives her father the pig anyway and leaves on a ship for the United States, where he meets and marries Sarah Miller. Elya and Sarah have a good marriage, despite the fact that they suffer from much bad luck. Elya never gives up looking for Madame Zeroni's son, who was also in the United States, because he feels guilty about not fulfilling his promise to her.

Stanley Yelnats II

Stanley Yelnats II is Stanley's great-grandfather, who made a lot of money in the stock market. Unfortunately, his stagecoach is robbed by Kissin' Kate Barlow when he is en route from New York to California. He is left stranded in the desert for three weeks. When asked how he survived, he always replies, "I found refuge on God's thumb" (the same mountain that Stanley and Zero climb). He later marries the nurse who takes care of him in the hospital and always blames his "no-good-pig-stealing-father" for his ordeal.

Katherine "Kissin' Kate" Barlow

Katherine Barlow is Green Lake's only schoolteacher. She is a very pretty and kind person. Everyone in the town loves her jarred peaches (the same jarred peaches that Zero and Stanley found under the boat named "Mary Lou"). Because the town's one-room schoolhouse needs repairs, Katherine trades her jarred peaches for the handiwork of Sam the Onion Man. During the time Sam makes the repairs to the schoolhouse, Katherine and Sam fall in love. At that time, a relationship between a black man and a white woman was illegal and unacceptable in Green Lake; the community members are intolerant. They destroy the schoolhouse and, as Sam and Katherine try to escape in his rowboat named after his donkey, Mary Lou, they kill Sam and rescue Katherine, against her wishes.

Three days later, Katherine shoots the town sheriff, who would not help her save Sam from the townspeople, and she becomes Kissin' Kate Barlow, a ruthless outlaw of the Wild West. Kissin' Kate Barlow kisses each man that she kills. She is vengeful and becomes an outlaw because of her grief and anger over the loss of Sam and the way the community members treated him. Kissin' Kate robs Stanley's great-grandfather as he rides a stagecoach to California. She doesn't kill him, but she leaves him stranded in the middle of the desert (near Green Lake).

Twenty years later, Kissin' Kate is living in the same cabin the Warden is living in today. Trout Walker and his wife break in to Kissin' Kate's cabin and intend to torture her until she tells them where she has stashed her loot. Instead of giving them an answer, Kissin' Kate is bitten by a yellow-spotted lizard and dies.

Sam the Onion Man

Sam is a black man in his early twenties who has an onion field on Green Lake. He has a beloved donkey named Mary Lou that pulls his cart full of onions through the streets of the community. Sam claims that his onions can cure anything and can even repel yellow-spotted lizards. Sam is quite skillful and soon begins making repairs on the schoolhouse for Katherine Barlow in exchange for her jarred peaches. They enjoy each other's company and soon fall in love. Because a relationship between a black man and a white woman was illegal at that time, the community takes the law into their own hands. Sam and his donkey are killed and, immediately thereafter, rain stops falling on Green Lake and the community does not survive.

Charles "Trout" Walker

Charles Walkers earns the nickname "Trout" because his feet smell like dead fish. (He has an incurable foot fungus that causes his feet to smell; it is the same foot odor problem that Clyde "Sweet Feet" Livingston has years later.) Trout is the son of a very wealthy man whose family owns most of the land on the east side of Green Lake when Green Lake is considered to be the largest lake in Texas. Trout is loud, stupid, arrogant, and disrespectful. He attends Katherine Barlow's evening class for adults in the one-room schoolhouse and consistently disrupts the lessons. Everyone is sure that Katherine will marry him because his family is wealthy, but she refuses even to ride on his motorized boat.

After Katherine is seen kissing Sam the Onion Man, Trout leads a mob of community members into the schoolhouse, which they destroy. When Katherine and Sam try to get away in Sam's rowboat, Trout's motorized boat runs into the rowboat and Sam is shot and killed.

Twenty years later, Katherine Barlow, then known as Kissin' Kate Barlow, is living in an abandoned cabin. Trout Walker and his wife, Linda Miller (whom the Warden resembles), break into Kissin' Kate's cabin and demand to know where she has hidden all the money that she has stolen. Kate indicates that she has buried the money in the dried-up lakebed. Trout's family, and future generations of Walkers, continue to dig, looking for Kissin' Kate's buried treasure for years.

Ms. Walker (The Warden)

The Warden is a tall woman with freckles and red hair. She wears black turquoise-studded boots (similar to the ones worn by Kissin' Kate Barlow years earlier). She is a descendant of Trout Walker and his wife Linda Miller. The Warden is a mysterious woman. She lives alone in a small cabin. She only seems to be interested in whether the boys have found something that has been buried in the dried-up lakebed. The buried treasure is the total focus of her life. The Warden will do anything to find it.

After Zero runs away, she has all of his files destroyed. She doesn't care about Zero. Her only concern is finding the buried treasure. She doesn't want her search halted for any reason. The Warden is a villainous and menacing person. She enforces the rules by threatening to scratch offenders with her nails, which are polished with rattlesnake venom. The Warden never gets the buried treasure. She is forced to close Camp Green Lake and sell her land, which eventually becomes a Girl Scout Camp.

Mr. Sir

Mr. Sir acts as the guard at Camp Green Lake. He wears a big cowboy hat and sunglasses and has a rattlesnake tattoo on his arm. He habitually eats sunflower seeds, which have replaced his habit of smoking cigarettes. Mr. Sir appears to be an extremely unhappy person. He is sarcastic and verbally abusive to the boys, always reminding them that they aren't attending a Girl Scout Camp. (Ironically, the camp does become a Girl Scout Camp at the novel's end.) Mr. Sir's actions are totally controlled by the Warden. Mr. Sir is humiliated when Stanley sees the Warden slap him (after she has painted her nails with rattlesnake venom) and hears the Warden tell him that she liked him better when he was smoking cigarettes than eating sunflower seeds (which he claims Stanley stole from his truck). Afterward, to show Stanley that he is in charge, he repeatedly neglects to fill Stanley's canteen with water. One day, Stanley is sure Mr. Sir put "some vile substance" in his canteen of water. By the time Stanley and Zero return to Camp Green Lake to dig up the suitcase, Mr. Sir is smoking cigarettes once again—an indication of a character weakness. Even though Mr. Sir appears intimidating to the boys at Camp Green Lake, his tough, mean demeanor is a façade. In fact, Mr. Sir is intimidated by the Warden and, therefore, does whatever she says.

Mr. Pendanski

Mr. Pendanski is the counselor for the boys in Group D. He has a shaved head and a "thick, curly black beard." The boys call him "Mom," and he calls each boy by his given name rather than by a nickname. He talks to the boys about their goals and dreams and about the importance of taking responsibility for their behaviors and actions. He wants the boys to become "useful and hardworking members of society." Mr. Pendanski, however, is morally ambiguous. He attempts to instill values and morality in the boys and then turns around and does the opposite. Whatever the Warden tells him to do, even if it means committing an illegal act (destroying Zero's file), he does it without question. Mr. Pendanski is a follower and not a leader.

X-Ray

X-Ray's name is pig latin for his given name, Rex. X-Ray wears glasses because he can't see very well, and he always uses the same shovel because he claims it is the shortest one (the holes dug by the boys are measured with their shovels). X-Ray is the unofficial leader of the boys in Group D. He is always first in line for lunch or to have his canteen refilled with water. X-Ray gives Stanley the nickname "Caveman." Stanley intimidates X-Ray because Stanley is bigger than he is and because Stanley is smart. For example, when Stanley gives X-Ray the gold tube he has found, he suggests that X-Ray wait until the next morning to show it to Mr. Pendanski, so that he can get more time off. To reward Stanley for his "loyalty," X-Ray tells Stanley to move up in line at the water truck.

After Zero begins digging half of Stanley's hole each day, X-Ray tells Stanley to be first in line because he is "better than all of us." Even though X-Ray appears to be sarcastic, there is a ring of truth to his words. Stanley takes the blame for the stolen sunflower seeds so the other boys will not get in trouble; he is also teaching Zero to read. In the end, when Stanley and Zero are back at Camp Green Lake, X-Ray acts as though he is jealous of Stanley—he is the only one of the group of boys who does not come over to talk to Stanley and Zero. Instead, he goes back to the Wreck Room alone.

Ms. Morengo

Ms. Morengo is a patent lawyer who is helping Stanley's father with a new product he has invented. After hearing about Stanley's case from his father, she investigates and finds proof that he has not stolen Clyde Livingston's sneakers. She has a court order from the judge who originally sentenced Stanley, releasing him from Camp Green Lake. She arrives at Camp Green Lake just as Stanley manages to climb out of the hole where he has found the buried suitcase.

Ms. Morengo is Hispanic. She has straight black hair and dark eyes. She speaks with a slight Mexican accent and she trills her r's. She is a short woman but she gives the impression that she is taller. She is self-confident and assertive, intimidated by neither the Attorney General nor the Warden. In fact, she threatens to sue them if anything happens to Stanley. Ms. Morengo has no tolerance for injustice, incompetence, or dishonesty.

Activities for Readers

1. Choose a scene from Holes and write a comic strip, including detailed illustrations.

2. The environment has a great effect on the characters in *Holes*. Using the Internet, find out whether the geography and weather Sachar describes in the novel are consistent with the actual geography and weather in Texas.

3. Stanley goes to court after he is arrested. As Stanley's attorney, write a closing argument persuading the jury of Stanley's innocence. Or write a closing argument as the prosecuting attorney, persuading the jury of Stanley's guilt.

4. Sachar includes tall-tales in *Holes*. Find out what tall-tales are and read a book of tall-tales, such as *Annie Oakley* or *Paul Bunyon*. Write a tall-tale of your own.

Additional Resources

Children's Literature Review. Vol. 28. Detroit: Gale Research, 1992: 200–205.

"Book Review: *Holes* by Louis Sachar." *Resource Room.* Online. www.resourceroom.net/comprehension/bookreviews/holes.htm.

"*Holes* Discussion Guide." *Scholastic.* Internet. teacher.scholastic.com/authorsandbooks/authors/sachar/activity.htm.

"Meet Louis Sachar." *Scholastic.* Internet. teacher.scholastic.com/authorsandbooks/authors/sachar/bio.htm.

"Meet the Author: Louis Sachar." Online. www.cbcbooks.org/columns/archives/sachar.htm.

Sachar, Louis. "Newbery Medal Acceptance Speech." *The Horn Book Magazine.* July–August 1999: 410–417.

Sachar, Sherre and Carla. "Louis Sachar." *The Horn Book Magazine.* July–August 1999: 418–422.

Strickland, Barbara. "Louis Sachar: Top of His Class." *The Austin Chronicle.* Online. www.auschron.com/issues/vol18/issue26/books.sachar.html.

"Sachar, Louis." *Educational Paperback Association.* Online. www.edupaperback.org/authorbios/sachar1.html.

OUT OF THE DUST (1998)

Life and Background of the Author

Karen Hesse is a poet and an author of books for children and young adults. She is perhaps best known for writing historical fiction—fiction that requires her to conduct detailed and meticulous research about another time and place, and then create a fictional story based on that research. Hesse does not just focus on the setting for her writing; she pays equal attention to the development of her characters. The protagonists in Hesse's writing are typically young, courageous, and determined females who discover ways to rise above adversity and tragedy. Through their trials and tribulations, Hesse portrays the power and endurance of the human spirit.

Hesse was born on August 29, 1952, in Baltimore, Maryland. Her childhood was not easy. She lived in a row house in an environment that did not include much privacy and, even though she was surrounded by people, she felt isolated. Her feelings of isolation spurred her to read, and her need for privacy led her to spend hours sitting on the boughs of an apple tree located out her back door, with a good book. Hesse loved to read, often getting into trouble for reading at night when she was supposed to be sleeping. As a child, one of her favorite authors was Dr. Seuss; later, author Katherine Paterson became another childhood favorite.

Hesse was a shy girl. She felt as though she was from another world, as though she never really belonged. She had friends, but she never felt close enough to them to trust them with her innermost secrets. Consequently, Hesse was lonely. Her world became the world she found in the books she read. Her reading also fueled her imagination. At one point during her childhood, her mother had to keep her from leaping from an upstairs window because Hesse believed she could fly.

Although Hesse had many thoughts about what she wanted to be when she grew up, her fifth grade teacher believed she could be a professional writer. Hesse never forgot her teacher's support and, because her teacher believed in her, Hesse believed in herself.

When Hesse's mother remarried, Hesse gained a stepfather and a stepsister. Initially, she was a bit jealous of the attention given her stepsister, who was a professional dancer. But with time, Hesse grew fond of both her stepfather and stepsister. To gain attention for herself, Hesse became interested in drama and began acting in school plays. She not only loved to act, but also proved to be an excellent actress. In 1969, she enrolled in Towson State College as a theater major. While in college, Hesse met Randy, her future husband, and because she felt she couldn't be in love and be in theater at the same time, she dropped out of theater, a decision she has never regretted.

Hesse and Randy eloped in 1971. She was 19 years old at the time. Soon after their marriage, Randy, who was in the Navy, was sent to Vietnam. While he was gone, Hesse lived in Norfolk, Virginia. During that time, she went back to school, attending the University of Maryland and graduating with a Bachelor of Arts degree in English and two minors: psychology and anthropology. She also continued to write poetry and became known for her poetry readings.

Over the years, Hesse had many jobs that later influenced her writing. She worked as a librarian, a substitute teacher, an advertising secretary, a proofreader, and a book reviewer, to name just a few of the jobs she has held.

In 1976, Hesse and her husband, who was home from Vietnam, took their pickup truck, some clothing, camping equipment, and two cats, and traveled across the United States for six months. When they drove into the state of Vermont, they knew they'd found their home. They ended up settling in Vermont and live in Southern Vermont today. Hesse and her husband had two daughters, one in 1979 and another in 1982, and motherhood became a priority and a demand on Hesse's time. As a result, she put poetry writing on hold. She did, however, begin to write children's books. Her first attempt was a story about a family's encounter with Bigfoot; the story was never published. Her second attempt began as a four-page story. After revising the story, it became a novel and was published in 1991 as *Wish on a Unicorn*, her first book. When her children became more independent, Hesse returned to writing poetry. She was rewarded for her efforts in 1998, when she won the Newbery Medal for *Out of the Dust*, a novel written entirely in free verse.

Hesse shares her writing with the members of her writing group and her daughters, who read her work and provide valuable feedback. She uses photographs discovered during her research, illustrating people who could be characters in the book she is writing, to help her develop realistic characters. Hesse never *creates* the bad things that happen to her characters; the bad things are true stories Hesse reads about while doing research for her book. Because Hesse writes historical fiction, she usually spends eight to ten months on extensive research for each book she writes. She spends a lot of time reading nonfiction, as research, and children's fiction.

Hesse does not reveal much about herself, but her books, which have received many awards and honors, tend to give her away. *Letters from Rifka* reveals that Hesse values independence as well as her Jewish heritage, *Phoenix Rising* portrays Hesse's love and respect for the land, *A Time of Angels* also shows the importance of Hesse's Jewish heritage, *The Music of Dolphins* shows that Hesse is willing to take chances, and *Out of the Dust* portrays Hesse's love of poetry.

Hesse's books are set in a specific place and time, covering serious topics. Her goal is to give her readers perspective, a different angle from which to view and understand life.

Hesse's Selected Works

Wish On a Unicorn (1991)

Letters from Rifka (1992)

Lavender (1993)

Lester's Dog (1993)

Poppy's Chair (1993)

Phoenix Rising (1994)

Sable (1994)

A Time of Angels (1995)

The Music of Dolphins (1996)

Out of the Dust (1997)

Just Juice (1998)

Come On, Rain! (1999)

Light in the Storm: The Civil War Diary of Amelia Martin (1999)

A Brief Synopsis

Literary
Device

Hesse narrates *Out of the Dust* in the first person, allowing Billie Jo Kelby, the protagonist, or main character, to describe her life from the winter of 1934 through the fall of 1935. Hesse writes the novel in free-verse poems, from firsthand fictionalized events, in the form of journal entries. The novel is historical. Hesse depicts the harsh reality of the

Oklahoma Panhandle during the Great Depression. The Oklahoma Panhandle, located in the southwestern Great Plains region of the United States, was known as the Dust Bowl. During the 1920s and 1930s, farmers plowed up grasslands to plant wheat. Drought, violent dust storms, and tornadoes that hit the area caused soil erosion. Consequently, the farmers and their families suffered unbelievable hardship and poverty.

Billie Jo is 14 years old when *Out of the Dust* begins. She lives near Joyce City, Oklahoma, located in the Oklahoma Panhandle, during the Great Depression of the 1930s, with her mother and father. Despite the continual dust storms, Billie Jo and her parents struggle to make the best of a grim situation by living their lives as normally as possible. Her father, a wheat farmer, works what is left of the farm and her mother, a tall, skinny, rather plain woman, spends the majority of her time cleaning house. Billie Jo helps Ma with the house cleaning, a chore that is never-ending because the dust and grit seeps into the house through every crack. Billie Jo's mother is pregnant. The baby's arrival is a long-awaited event that her family is looking forward to.

Character Insight

Overall, Billie Jo is quite content. She is able to attend school regularly and is the top eighth-grade student in the state of Oklahoma, according to the results of a statewide test. She is saddened when her best friend Livvie leaves the Dust Bowl and moves to California with her family and when rabbits are killed because they are eating farmers' crops, the only vegetation left for them to eat. Billie Jo's joy in life is to play the piano. Her mother, an accomplished pianist, taught her to play when Billie Jo was only five years old. Although she doesn't play as well as her mother, Billie Jo puts her heart into her music and plays a "fierce" piano.

Literary Device

When Arley Wanderdale, the music teacher at Billie Jo's school, asks her to play the piano at the Palace Theatre with his band, the Black Mesa Boys, and Mad Dog Craddock (a singer and friend to Billie Jo), she is ecstatic. Ma gives her permission to play, and Billie Jo feels like she is in heaven. To Billie Jo, there is nothing better than playing the piano while the audience snaps their fingers, taps their feet, and sways to the music. Billie Jo is an excellent entertainer, and Arley Wanderdale knows it. He asks Billie Jo to travel to neighboring towns with him and the Black Mesa Boys during the summer months. Billie Jo's mother reluctantly agrees to let her go because she will be supervised by Vera, Arley's wife, and will be earning a little money—something Billie Jo's family desperately needs.

In July, Billie Jo's life changes dramatically as a result of a horrific accident. Her father leaves a pail of kerosene next to the stove. Thinking it is a pail of water, her mother picks it up to make her father some coffee. The kerosene immediately catches fire. Her mother runs outside to get her father, and Billie Jo—trying to save the house from going up in flames—throws the flaming pail of kerosene out the door. The pail of flaming kerosene splashes onto her mother, who is right in its path. Billie Jo uses her hands to beat out the flames that engulf her mother. Billie Jo's hands are badly burned and her mother, suffering from severe burns, dies giving birth to a baby boy a month later. The baby only lives a few days, and Billie Jo names her dead brother Franklin (after President Franklin Delano Roosevelt). Franklin is buried in his mother's arms.

Billie Jo grieves for her mother and baby brother. She is in pain both emotionally and physically. She feels guilty because she blames herself for their deaths. She blames her father, too, and is angry with him for leaving the kerosene next to the stove. She questions whether she can ever forgive him—or herself. Billie Jo takes over her mother's chores, but because her hands are so badly burned, she is in agony. The physical pain she experiences is so great that it prevents her from playing the piano. Billie Jo's father is also grieving. He has lost his wife and son and is losing his farm and crops. He becomes depressed and withdrawn, treating Billie Jo as though she is invisible. He is unable to comfort or reassure her, and they become strangers living under the same roof. Her father deals with his grief by digging a big hole for an eventual pond, following through on a suggestion that Billie Jo's mother had provided weeks ago. He soon takes a job working long hours for Wireless Power.

Life goes on for Billie Jo and her father. Dust storms and the aftermath have become a common occurrence. Billie Jo is lonely. Most people feel sorry for her because she is motherless. She has few friends and is grateful to Mad Dog, because he sees her for who she is and treats her as friend, not as a pitiful victim.

After hearing about a talent contest hosted by the Palace Theatre, Billie Jo decides to enter. She practices on the piano at school, unable to play on her mother's piano at home because her feelings of guilt and her grief consume her. While competing in the contest, Billie Jo plays her heart out and wins third prize, but not without paying a price—her hands "scream with pain for days." Billie Jo tries to play the piano again, but she can't; she feels like a "cripple." Her father begins to take adult education classes at night, just in case the farm doesn't make it and he has to make a living some other way. Billie Jo receives a letter from Aunt Ellis inviting her to live in Lubbock, Texas. Billie Jo puts the letter on the shelf over her mother's piano, as a reminder that she has an escape from the Dust Bowl.

Character Insight

Noticing that her father has spots on his skin that look just like *his* father's skin cancer, Billie Jo decides to leave before her father leaves her (she is afraid he will die of skin cancer). She jumps on a freight train and travels in a boxcar as far as Flagstaff, Arizona. Her intention is to get out of the Dust Bowl and never go back. On her journey, she realizes that she cannot get "out of the dust" because the dust is a part of her. She is able to feel compassion for her father, to understand his grief, and to forgive him and ultimately forgive herself. She returns home with a deeper understanding of her father and herself.

Billie Jo and her father redefine their relationship and once again become a family. Her father meets Louise, a teacher at the night school he attended, and she becomes a special person in his life. Billie Jo is able to accept Louise as part of their family and understands that spirit, hopes, and dreams can be rekindled with love.

Character Web

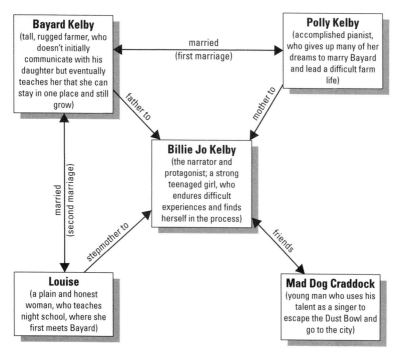

Geographical Map

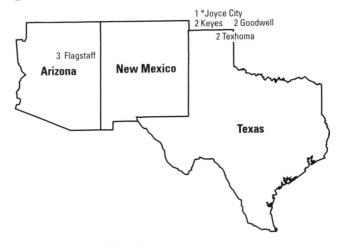

1. Joyce City, Oklahoma. Town that Billie Jo lives near.

2. Keyes, Oklahoma; Goodwell, Oklahoma; Texhoma, Texas. Billie Joe travels to these cities with Arley Wanderdale and the Black Mesa Boys to play piano.

3. Flagstaff, Arizona. Billie Jo runs away from home by jumping on a freight train. She takes the train as far as Flagstaff, Arizona, realizes her home is with her Pa, and returns to Joyce City.

Major Themes

Major themes in *Out of the Dust* include loss and forgiveness, family, and the environment. Hesse's thematic messages convey the power of the human spirit to endure and transcend the pain that accompanies adversity and tragedy.

Throughout the novel, loss and grief (which is a reaction to loss) are predominant themes. Billie Jo and her father suffer multiple losses throughout the novel. Billie Jo loses her best friend, Livvie, when Livvie's family moves to California to get away from the dust. Billie Jo loses her mother and newborn baby brother when they die. Billie Jo misses her mother terribly. She cleans the dust and mud out of the house because her mother would have cleaned if she were alive. She regrets that she put off doing things with her mother, such as going through her boxes of memorabilia. She thinks about talking to her mother about daily occurrences, but then, "she remembers," remembers that her mother is dead. People blame Billie Jo for her mother's death, causing Billie Jo to lose self-respect (another loss) and to blame herself.

Billie Jo's hands are badly burned as a result of the accident. She tried to beat out the flames on her mother. Her hands are scarred; to stretch her fingers to play the piano is agony. Billie Jo experiences the loss of her ability to play the piano and the loss of her self-esteem. People no longer see Billie Jo the talented pianist, but instead they feel sorry for her and see the "poor motherless thing."

Style & Language

Billie Jo is grieving and when people grieve, it is natural for them to feel anger. Billie Jo is very angry. She says,

I am so filled with bitterness,

it comes from the dust, it comes

from the silence of my father, it comes

from the absence of Ma.

Character Insight

She is motherless and she blames herself and her father. She is angry because her father has distanced himself from her. She is angry because she can't play the piano the way she used to. And she is angry because she can no longer depend on her piano playing as her ticket out of the Dust Bowl.

As Billie Jo works through her grief, she begins to accept what happened. She knows now that her father was not able to reassure or comfort her because he was grieving, too. And, the reason he left his wife's bedside to go to a bar while she was sick was because he couldn't bear the pain of losing her. Billie Jo understands that her father did the best he could at the time. In spite of overwhelming losses, Billie Jo is able to forgive herself and her father.

Billie Jo's father is also able to forgive. He loses his wife and new-born son when they die. He loses his crops and his livelihood because of the drought and dust storms. And he loses his daughter when Billie Jo runs away. While Billie Jo is gone, her father gains insight into their situation, resulting in reconciliation with his daughter and a redefining of their family.

Theme

Family is another major theme in the novel. Billie Jo's family changes dramatically as the story progresses. Her mother and father always wanted more children; finally, Billie Jo's mother is pregnant. They do "normal" family things. Her father farms and her mother cooks, bakes, and makes sure that Billie Jo gets her homework completed. After the accident, after Billie Jo's mother and newborn baby brother die, there is a huge void in her life and in her father's life. They sit across the table from each other, but it is as though they are strangers. They are family, but their family is going through a transition. The family they knew has been destroyed. When Billie Jo returns home after having run away, she and her father talk. They realize they are connected. They redefine their relationship and their family. They finally become comfortable with each other again and are able to include Louise, the woman Billie Jo's father becomes engaged to, in their family.

Style & Language

The environment and the effect the environment has on the people living in the Dust Bowl is a third major theme. The drought that takes place in the Dust Bowl and the resulting dust storms cause poverty because the wheat crops are destroyed. The poverty, in turn, decreases morale and causes the people to become depressed. Living in the Dust Bowl under these conditions creates tremendous hardships. Animals die because there is nothing for them to eat or drink and there is dirt and dust everywhere. Billie Jo's father exhibits a sense of humor commenting that, "the potatoes were peppered plenty," and how lucky they were because they were having "chocolate" milk to drink. The "pepper" is dust, and the milk looks like chocolate milk because of the dust.

The environment also causes people to be fearful. Billie Jo expresses her fears when she asks,

Where would we be without

somewhere to live?

Without some work to do?

Without something to eat?

And yet, in spite of the extremely difficult living conditions, the people stay and farm the land—and they are happy. Hesse portrays the pain that exists in life and the joy that human beings are capable of feeling when the suffering is over and they are able to forgive and be surrounded by the love of family. By setting the novel in the Dust Bowl, Hesse allows readers to appreciate their own present-day environment.

About the Characters

Billie Jo Kelby

Billie Jo Kelby is the strong and courageous protagonist, or main character, of the novel. She is 14 years old when the story begins, tall and slender, with red hair and freckles, and she loves apples. She is a dynamic character. Her experiences and actions cause her to change during the novel. We know how Billie Jo changes because Hesse narrates *Out of the Dust* in the first person, allowing Billie Jo to speak for herself.

When the novel begins, Billie Jo is making the best of her life despite the dust storms, depression, and drought. She attends school and does well, receiving the highest score in the state on the standardized state test for eighth graders. She also plays a "fierce" piano. Playing the piano is Billie Jo's passion. When she plays, she gets lost in the music. She is self-confident about her ability to play the piano and loves to entertain at the Palace Theatre with Arley Wanderdale and his band, the Black Mesa Boys, and singer and friend, Mad Dog Craddock. Billie Jo envisions herself moving away from the Dust Bowl someday; her means of escape will be her talent as a pianist.

After the accident, when Billie Jo throws the burning pail of kerosene out the door of the house and onto her mother, and after the death of her mother and newborn baby brother, Billie Jo's life changes forever. She is in extreme physical pain because her hands are badly burned. Her hands are scarred and curled up, making it painful for her to stretch her fingers and play the piano. Billie Jo is in emotional pain as well. She is grieving for the loss of her mother, her baby brother, and her ability to play the piano, which was to be her escape out of the Dust Bowl. Billie Jo has also temporarily lost her father. He has unknowingly abandoned her. He is grieving also and, as a result, is distant and self-absorbed, incapable of paying attention to Billie Jo. These losses contribute to Billie Jo's loneliness and isolation. Billie Jo also feels angry towards her father for having left the pail of kerosene in the kitchen in the first place. She wonders if she can ever forgive him.

Feeling guilty and despondent, Billie Jo runs away. Her journey, on a freight train, takes her to Flagstaff, Arizona. She confronts her misery and begins to accept herself as being "her father's daughter." She knows that "the dust is a part of her as it is a part of her father." She realizes that her father didn't turn his back on her intentionally; he was grieving as she was. Billie Jo returns home—able to forgive herself and her father. She is able to give herself permission to exercise her hands by playing her mother's piano once again.

Bayard Kelby

Bayard is Billie Jo's father. He stands tall, has "blondy-red hair and . . . high cheeks rugged with wind." (Billie Jo closely resembles him.) Although Hesse does not directly reveal his thoughts and feelings throughout the novel, she portrays Bayard's character through the observances of Billie Jo. Bayard is an uncommunicative man. He was a dutiful husband and never falters in his role as a dutiful father to Billie Jo.

Bayard is a wheat farmer. He continues to work the farm despite the fact that he hasn't had a profitable crop in years. He never gives up hope that it will rain and the ground will become fertile again. In this way, Bayard is like Job, who is written about in the Old Testament of the Bible. Job was stripped of all his earthly possessions—his farm, his house, and his family. Even though he had nothing, Job never turned his back on God or blamed God for his misfortune. He maintained his faith and received great rewards. Like Job, Bayard is slowly losing his farm and has lost his wife and son, but he never loses faith that the rain will come again and his farm will prosper. He will never leave the Dust Bowl. Billie Jo understands that "he and the land have a hold on each other."

When Billie Jo returns home after running away, Bayard's relationship with her changes. He begins to pay attention to her and they work at becoming a family again. They begin to talk to each other and Bayard goes to Doc Rice to have the cancer removed from his skin, evidence that he is not giving up hope. Bayard meets Louise, a teacher at the night school where he was taking classes (just in case he needed something to fall back on), and he and Billie Jo include her in their family. He teaches Billie Jo that "you can stay in one place and still grow."

Polly Kelby (Pol)

Pol is Billie Jo's mother. Billie Jo describes her as being "long and skinny, with poor teeth, and dark hair always needing a wash." Although Hesse does not reveal Pol's past, Billie Jo implies that her mother sacrificed a great deal to live in the Dust Bowl with Bayard. She is an accomplished pianist and taught Billie Jo how to play the piano at the age of five. As Bayard's wife, she adapts. She understands and accepts her husband's uncommunicative nature and the conditions that accompany living in the Dust Bowl.

Pol is stoic—restrained and unflappable. When Billie Jo tells her that she has received the highest grade in the state on the eighth-grade standardized test, Pol's response is, "I knew you could." Billie Jo knows her mother is pleased about her accomplishment, but Pol doesn't show it the way other mothers do. Pol is also stubborn and proud. In spite of the constant dust storms, she works hard to keep her house clean. She scrub floors, beats the furniture and rugs, and washes clothes over and over again without seeming to tire of the repetitious, hard work. She grows two apple trees in the front yard, in the midst of the drought, and understands that crops besides wheat will have to be grown in order for the farm—and the family—to survive.

Pol suffers horribly after being burned when Billie Jo throws the burning kerosene out the door and accidentally onto her. She dies after giving birth to a baby boy, who also dies days later. They are buried together on the farm.

Louise

Louise will marry Billie Jo's father and become Billie Jo's stepmother. Louise is a "plain and honest" woman. She teaches the night school class Billie Jo's father takes, and keeps her father company when Billie Jo runs away on the freight train. Louise is understanding of the difficult times that Billie Jo and her father have been through during the past year. She accepts her role as a newcomer to the family and is patient. She doesn't push Billie Jo to talk, change, or do anything Billie Jo is not ready to do.

Mad Dog Craddock

Mad Dog is Billie Jo's friend. He was named Mad Dog because, when he was a child, he bit everyone. He is an attractive boy with blue eyes. Mad Dog lives in the Dust Bowl and works on a farm as a "plow-boy." He has a "smooth voice" and sings with Arley Wanderdale and his band, the Black Mesa Boys.

Mad Dog respects Billie Jo and sees her as "Billie Jo Kelby," the person and musician, not the "motherless" child that others seem to see first. Mad Dog doesn't feel sorry for Billie Jo, and he is not embarrassed by her scarred hands or the accident that she was involved in that culminated in her mother's death.

Mad Dog escapes the Dust Bowl by getting a job in Amarillo as a radio performer. If Billie Jo's hands had not been severely burned in the accident, she might have followed in Mad Dog's footsteps and used her talent as a pianist to escape as well.

Activities for Readers

1. Research the Dust Bowl. Create a list of facts that includes the number and names of the states that were affected, the worst years, and any other significant information.

2. Billie Jo and others living in the Dust Bowl relied on music for entertainment. Research musicians and music that were popular during the 1930s.

3. Billie Jo's mother sends her to the store with fifty cents to buy ingredients for a cake. Using the library or the Internet, find out what items actually cost during the 1930s. Go to the grocery store and compare the price of each item to the price of the same item today.

4. Throughout the novel, we are not privy to Billie Jo's father's feelings. Write a journal entry from his point of view, expressing his feelings and thoughts about the drought, his farm, the death of his wife and son, and/or his daughter who has run away.

5. Write a poem that is a portrait of a photograph of your choosing. Be sure to include similes, metaphors, and adjectives.

Additional Resources

Bowen, Brenda. "Karen Hesse." *The Horn Book*. July–August 1998: 428–432.

Children's Literature Review. Vol. 54. Detroit: Gale Research, 1999: 26–42.

Hesse, Karen. "Newbery Medal Acceptance." *The Horn Book*. July–August 1998: 422–427.

"Interview Transcript." *Scholastic*. Online. teacher.scholastic.com/authorsandbooks/authors/hesse/tscript.htm.

Littlejohn, Nancy. "Children's Book Reviews." *Writers Write: The Internet Writing Journal*. Online. www.writerswrite.com/journal/may98/child2.htm.

"Meet Karen Hesse." *Scholastic*. Internet. teacher.scholastic.com/authorsandbooks/authors/hesse/bio.htm.

THE VIEW FROM SATURDAY (1997)

Life and Background of the Author

Elaine Lobl Konigsburg is the author and illustrator of humorous, thought-provoking novels and stories for adolescents and young children. She has won the Newbery Medal twice—first for *From the Mixed-Up Files of Mrs. Basil E. Frankweiler* (1967), and then for *A View From Saturday* (1991). In 1967, Konigsburg's novel *Jennifer, Hecate, Macbeth, William McKinley, and Me, Elizabeth* (1967) was named a Newbery Honor Book. Konigsburg is the only author to have one book win a Newbery Medal and another book receive a Newbery honor in the same year. Konigsburg's books are amusing; however, they include a serious element that usually relates to an adolescent's search for the answer to the question, "Who am I?" Her protagonists are witty, intelligent, articulate characters. Konigsburg writes about a wide variety of topics in many different genres, including historical fiction, contemporary realism, fantasy, and picture books for children.

Konigsburg was born on February 10, 1930, in New York City, to Adolph Lobl, a businessman, and Beulah Klein. She was the second of three daughters. Konigsburg didn't grow up in New York City. Instead, she spent most of her childhood living with her family in small towns in Pennsylvania. As a child, Konigsburg was a voracious reader. Most of the time, she read in the bathroom of her house, because it was the only room that had a lock on the door and because she could run water to hide the fact that she was crying over a sentimental scene in a book. Konigsburg admits that she read a lot of "trashy" books during her childhood and adolescence. Her favorite books however, were *Charlotte's Web* and *Stuart Little* by E.B. White and *Pride and Prejudice* and *Sense and Sensibility* by Jane Austen. Konigsburg did exceptionally well in her school courses and graduated as valedictorian from Farrell High School.

During the year after high school, Konigsburg worked as a bookkeeper in a wholesale meat plant. David Konigsburg, a brother of one of the owners of the meat plant, visited the office and he and Elaine became friendly. When she finally had enough money for her first year of college, Konigsburg enrolled in Carnegie Institute of Technology in Pittsburgh as a chemistry major. She was the first person in her family to go to college. In 1952, she graduated with honors and received a Bachelor of Science degree. She married David Konigsburg on July 6, 1952. While her husband studied psychology at the University of Pittsburgh, Konigsburg pursued her studies in chemistry. She attended graduate school at the University of Pittsburgh until 1954.

After her husband completed his doctoral degree in psychology, the couple moved to Jacksonville, Florida. Konigsburg got a job teaching science at Bartram, a private school for girls. While teaching, she became more interested in the uncomfortable feelings the adolescents were experiencing than in the science classes themselves. She quit teaching in 1955, a short time before her son Paul was born. A year later, after her daughter, Laurie, was born, Konigsburg took up painting. In 1959, her third child, Ross, was born. The following year, Konigsburg returned to teaching part-time. She taught for two years, and, in 1962, her family moved to the metropolitan New York area. When her younger son started school, Konigsburg began writing. Her first two books, *Jennifer, Hecate, Macbeth, William McKinley, and Me, Elizabeth* and *From the Mixed-Up Files of Mrs. Basil E. Frankweiler,* were published in 1967. Konigsburg and her family moved back to Jacksonville, Florida, in 1968. In the middle of moving, she found out that *From the Mixed-Up Files of Mrs. Basil E. Frankweiler* was a Newbery Medal winner and *Jennifer, Hecate, Macbeth, William McKinley, and Me, Elizabeth* was named a Newbery Honor Book.

Since winning her first Newbery Medal Award, Konigsburg has written and illustrated numerous books. Her audience is mostly made up of junior high school students or students in late elementary school. Her writing has received much acclaim. Twenty-nine years after winning her first Newbery Medal, Konigsburg won her second Newbery Medal Award, this time for *The View From Saturday.*

Today, Konigsburg lives in Ponte Vedra Beach, Florida, with her husband, David. When she isn't writing, she enjoys reading, drawing, painting, and walking on the beach.

Konigsburg's Selected Works

Jennifer, Hecate, Macbeth, William McKinley, and Me, Elizabeth (1967)

From the Mixed-up Files of Mrs. Basil E. Frankweiler (1967)

About the B'Nai Bagels (1969)

(George) (1970)

Altogether, One at a Time (1971)

A Proud Taste for Scarlet and Miniver (1973)

The Dragon in the Ghetto Caper (1974)

The Second Mrs. Giaconda (1975)

Father's Arcane Daughter (1976)

Throwing Shadows (1979)

Journey to an 800 Number (1982)

Up From Jericho Tel (1986)

The Mask Beneath the Face: Reading About and With, Writing About and for Children (1990)

Samuel Todd's Book of Great Colors (1990)

Samuel Todd's Book of Great Inventions (1991)

Amy Elizabeth Explores Bloomingdale's (1992)

T-Backs, T-Shirts, COAT, and Suit (1993)

TalkTalk: A Children's Book Author Speaks to Grown-Ups (1995)

The View From Saturday (1996)

Silent to the Bone (2000)

A Brief Synopsis

Konigsburg writes *The View From Saturday* in shifting points of view. The third person omniscient viewpoint is used to relate the thoughts and feelings of all the characters. The third person limited omniscient viewpoint focuses on, and is limited to, Mrs. Olinski's thoughts and feelings. Finally, Konigsburg uses the first person point of view to allow each protagonist to relate his or her thoughts and feelings as they tell their story.

Literary Device

The framework of the novel is the Academic Bowl competition and Mrs. Olinski's journey. Intertwined within this framework are the stories of the personal journeys of Noah, Nadia, Ethan, and Julian. The stories integrate the past with the present and fit together like a giant jigsaw puzzle. Konigsburg does not portray just one protagonist, but five—Mrs. Olinski, Noah, Nadia, Ethan, and Julian—all of whom unite to reach a common goal.

Literary Device

Noah is sent to Century Village, a retirement community in Florida, to stay with his grandparents, Nate and Sadie Gershom, while his parents go on a vacation. While Noah is visiting his grandparents, two other residents of Century Village, Margaret Draper and Izzy Diamondstein, decide to get married. Noah's grandparents volunteer to help with the wedding preparations: His grandmother will bake the cake and his grandfather will supply the music by playing his violin. Noah gets involved in the preparations when he offers to help another resident, Tillie Nachman, with the invitations. Tillie teaches Noah calligraphy and everything is going well until the cat spills the ink onto five invitations. To rectify the situation, Noah comes up with the idea that prizes will be awarded to the people who receive the invitations with the ink spills—but he doesn't know just yet what the prizes will be.

Noah also helps gather the groceries needed for the food that is being made for the reception and uses his wagon to transport flowers to the clubhouse. He is going to transport the wedding cake to the clubhouse as well, when Allen Diamondstein (Izzy's son and Nadia's father) slips on water and causes the cake to topple over. Allen, who is supposed to be his father's best man, must go to the emergency room (where he learns he has sprained his ankle). Noah offers to take his place and be the best man for the wedding.

Theme

At the reception, Noah must come up with prizes for the ink-stained invitations. He has no choice but "to give up things he loved." He only has four gifts, so he decides that the fifth gift is for one of the recipients to give his or her gift away to someone else. Soon, all of Noah's "gifts kept on giving." Noah discovers kindness in himself and in others.

Character Insight

Meanwhile, Nadia goes to Florida, with her dog Ginger, to visit her father, Allen Diamondstein, who is living in a "swinging-singles apartment complex." Nadia's parents recently divorced and Nadia moved to Epiphany, New York, with her mother. Nadia's relationship with her father is shaky, mainly because he doesn't know how to treat her. Allen hovers over Nadia, and she can't stand it. They spend time with her grandfather, Izzy Diamondstein, and his new wife, Margaret Draper. Izzy and Margaret walk the beach every morning and evening to rescue sea turtles and help them survive, and Allen and Nadia join them.

Theme

Nadia knows quite a bit about sea turtles because she wrote a paper about them for school. She resents the fact that her father asks Margaret questions about the sea turtles and not her. When Ethan, Margaret's grandson, shows up, Nadia feels more left out and refuses to walk the beach or visit her grandparents. Finally, Nadia and her father talk. Nadia is able to see that both she and her father have been going through difficult times and need to adjust to their new living arrangements (life without each other living under the same roof all the time). Nadia sees parallels between her life and the life of the sea turtles. She and her father agree to help and support each other and to "give each other a lift between switches."

Ethan Potter, Margaret Draper's grandson, lives on a farm in Epiphany with his parents. He goes to Florida to visit his grandmother at the same time Nadia is in Florida visiting her father and grandfather. Because Ethan and Nadia share grandparents now, they meet each other in Florida and spend time together.

Character Insight

On the first day of school, Ethan stakes out his seat on the school bus, wanting to have the seat to himself. But Julian Singh, a new student in school, chooses to sit next to him on the bus. Ethan tries to avoid conversation and eye contact with Julian, but Julian's kindness toward Ethan and everyone else influences Ethan. Ethan realizes that bullies from school intend to harass Julian, so he protects Julian from harm.

Literary Device

Julian Singh has just moved to Epiphany with his father. They bought the Sillington House and intend to open a Bed and Breakfast inn. Because Julian is new in Epiphany, and because he is different (he speaks with a British accent and is almost always polite and cheerful), he doesn't have any friends. Julian invites Noah, Nadia, and Ethan to the Sillington House for tea. The four friends call themselves "The Souls" and begin to meet at the Sillington House each Saturday at four o'clock for tea.

Julian's life at Epiphany is not easy. He is made fun of by mean students. Julian saves Nadia's dog, and the dog of his enemy's friend from a practical joke. He manages to find kindness in spite of the malice that he must endure.

The overall framework, the story that holds the stories of Noah, Nadia, Ethan, and Julian together, is Mrs. Olinski's story. Mrs. Olinski has returned to teaching after a ten-year absence. She is a paraplegic and is teaching her sixth grade class from a wheelchair. She endures discrimination and harassment from people who are ignorant about what it means to be physically handicapped.

Theme

Mrs. Olinski appoints Noah, Nadia, Ethan, and Julian to be on her Academic Bowl team. When she appoints them, she is unaware that they are The Souls. The team makes it all the way to the state finals and becomes champion. At the conclusion of her journey, Mrs. Olinski discovers kindness once again both within herself and within others. Konigsburg concludes the novel with an ambiguous question: Did The Souls choose to be on the Academic Bowl team, or did Mrs. Olinski choose *them*?

Character Map

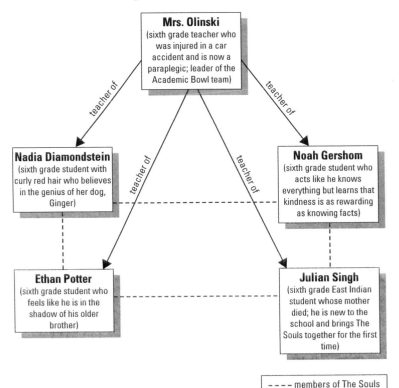

Mrs. Olinski
(sixth grade teacher who was injured in a car accident and is now a paraplegic; leader of the Academic Bowl team)

teacher of

teacher of

teacher of

teacher of

Nadia Diamondstein
(sixth grade student with curly red hair who believes in the genius of her dog, Ginger)

Noah Gershom
(sixth grade student who acts like he knows everything but learns that kindness is as rewarding as knowing facts)

Ethan Potter
(sixth grade student who feels like he is in the shadow of his older brother)

Julian Singh
(sixth grade East Indian student whose mother died; he is new to the school and brings The Souls together for the first time)

- - - - members of The Souls

Genealogy

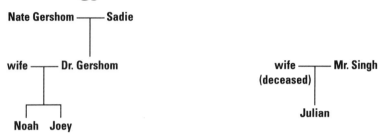

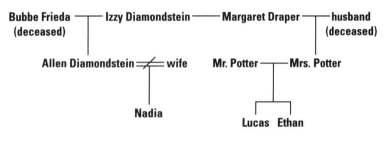

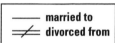

————— married to
⧸⧸ divorced from

Major Themes

According to Konigsburg, the theme that unites the stories in *The View From Saturday* is "kindness and the courage it takes to be kind." After winning the state championship of the Academic Bowl, Mr. Singh tells Mrs. Olinski that "The Souls have all returned from a journey. . . . Noah found something at Century Village; Nadia on the Sargasso Sea; Ethan on the bus. . . ." and Julian, who had the longest journey of all, at Epiphany Middle School. Mr. Singh tells Mrs. Olinski that she found the same thing at Sillington House that The Souls found on their journey—kindness in others and the ability to see it in themselves.

Character Insight

Through Mr. Singh, Konigsburg explains her notion, "that the human brain must be jump-started with experience. . . ." Konigsburg asks whether or not a person can possibly know kindness if he or she has never been treated with kindness. She concludes that if people have never known kindness, they are not aware it is absent from their lives. By understanding and appreciating kindness in others, The Souls are able to develop kindness within themselves. Their kindness enables them to help others, which binds them together as friends. For example, when presented with cruelty, The Souls take action. Ethan protects Julian from bullies; Julian protects Nadia's dog, as well as his enemy's dog, from harm; and all four of The Souls protect Mrs. Olinski from being mistreated.

The bond of friendship that develops between the members of The Souls portrays the interdependence, or teamwork, that cannot function without respect, trust, acceptance, and courtesy. The Souls' team work is exhibited when each member of The Souls puts an arm in the air or a leg in the aisle in their classroom—without having spoken to each other ahead of time—to signify their commitment to support Mrs. Olinski. Mrs. Olinski comments about The Souls and the way they "seemed to communicate with a secret stealth language that slipped beneath thought." After defeating Knightsbridge in the Academic Bowl, The Souls again seem to be thinking as one:

Ethan said, "Look, Ma, no hands," and Noah said, "Look, Ma, no legs," and Nadia thought, "Sometimes people need a lift between switches," and Julian said nothing but rubbed the little ivory monkey in his pocket.

The Souls made a commitment to support Mrs. Olinski, and they live up to their commitment.

Theme

Sensitivity to social issues in society is another major theme in *The View From Saturday*. Konigsburg presents the concept of diversity, from the viewpoint of educators, as a fad—something that is only temporarily important or popular. Dr. Rohmer, the District Superintendent of Clarion County, feels enlightened because he has attended a workshop on multiculturalism. He ignorantly informs Mrs. Olinski that "Jews, half-Jews, and WASPs have nothing to do with diversity." Other groups, such as East Indians and handicapped people, also seem to be excluded from diversity. Konigsburg portrays the educators who advocate diversity as people who are using the issue for their own personal advancement rather than for the advancement of diverse groups in society.

Another social issue that Konigsburg portrays is the change that has taken place in the way young people view education, adults, and peers. Mrs. Olinski is shocked to realize that her sixth graders don't seem to be interested in learning. They ask "So what?" instead of "Now what?" When Mrs. Olinski explains to her class that she is a paraplegic, an insensitive student writes the word "cripple" on the chalkboard during the lunch break. Even though Mrs. Olinski's observations allude to the overall impression that sixth graders, and the majority of students in general, do not care about learning, Konigsburg does not leave out the sixth graders who *do* care about learning. The Souls, members of the Academic Bowl team, spend their free time studying and drilling for the competition. They inspire other students to become involved in the Academic Bowl as spectators because their school is accomplishing an unexpected feat. Suddenly, knowledge becomes popular.

Through the unique journey that each character experiences, Konigsburg explores the question that every human being asks during the course of a lifetime: "Who am I?" She also depicts the interdependence that exists between people as well as the responsibility that everyone has to show kindness to others. Konigsburg also conveys her hope for understanding of all diverse groups and the importance of education.

About the Characters

Each of the five characters listed below is a central character in *The View From Saturday*. The characters each take a spiritual journey in which they discover kindness within themselves and within others. Because the characters change as a result of personal experiences and actions, they are *dynamic* characters.

Eva Marie Olinski

Eva Marie Olinski is a sixth-grade teacher at Epiphany Middle School. She is nervous on the first day of school because she hasn't taught in years and because she is now in a wheelchair. Ten years ago, Mrs. Olinski was in an automobile accident. Her husband was killed and she was paralyzed from the waist down.

Over the years, Mrs. Olinski has accepted her disability and has become self-confident enough in her wheelchair to try teaching again. However, she is aware of the reaction she gets from other people; they stare at her and treat her as though she is "different." This reaction causes Mrs. Olinski to feel self-conscious. The environment at Epiphany Middle School is quite hostile toward Mrs. Olinski. She is called a "cripple" and is treated disrespectfully. She feels sympathy for people who don't understand that "'cripples' are a diverse group of people" with thoughts and feelings.

At times, Mrs. Olinski is reminded of her physical limitations and of the losses she has endured. She lost her husband, the use of her legs, and the hopes and dreams she shared with her husband of having a family of their own. At Sillington House, Mrs. Olinski is "blinded by jealousy" when she sees Mrs. Draper (Mrs. Diamondstein now), her former principal, hug her grandson, Ethan. But instead of hanging on to that anger, Mrs. Olinski explores her feelings and, because she is in the company of people who accept her, feels her burden "lift from her shoulders."

When Mrs. Olinski appoints her academic team, she begins her journey to find meaning in her life once again and to discover kindness in others. With the support of The Souls, she feels less timid, she is able to maintain balance in the classroom, and she can relax when she is at Sillington House because The Souls and Mr. Singh don't pay any attention to her paralysis or her wheelchair.

At the novel's conclusion, Mrs. Olinski feels "a sense of loss" after her academic team is victorious. Mr. Singh points out to her that it is important to stop and enjoy the moment of victory.

Nadia Diamondstein

Nadia is a sixth-grade student at Epiphany Middle School. She is chubby, has freckles on her nose, and bright red curly hair. Nadia is totally devoted to her dog, Ginger, who she believes is a "genius." Because of her parents' recent divorce, Nadia moves to New York state with her mother. Her mother, who is originally from New York, gets a job working for Noah's father, a dentist. Nadia's father stays in Florida, sells the house they lived in, and moves to a "swinging-singles apartment complex."

Nadia's life has changed completely. Because everything is new, nothing is familiar to her. She has not made new friends in New York yet, and when she tries to see old friends when she visits her father in Florida, it is a chore to make arrangements to get together. Consequently, Nadia chooses Ginger's company. Nadia feels that "inside [her] there [is] a lot of best friendship that no one but Ginger [is] using." She also feels left out and unimportant. Nobody told Nadia that Margaret Draper (her grandfather's new wife) had arranged her mother's job interview with Dr. Gershom in Epiphany. "No one seemed to think that it would matter to [her] where [she] lived" or that she would have to commute between her parents. When she visits her father, her father doesn't ask *her* about the sea turtles (Nadia had written a paper for school about the sea turtles and received an A on the paper), he asks Margaret. And later, when a nest of sea turtles hatches, Nadia's grandfather hugs and congratulates Margaret, Ethan, and her father—but not Nadia.

Nadia's journey parallels her life and the life cycle of the sea turtles. Both Nadia and the sea turtles have parents who are not physically present, they must endure a long maturation process, and they face the possibility along the way of losing their sense of direction and not having any help. By comparing the life cycle of the sea turtles to her life with divorced parents, Nadia is able to gain insight and understanding. Like the sea turtles, Nadia and her father have been picked up and put down in unfamiliar surroundings due to a "storm in their private lives. . . . They have been stranded and both need help resettling." After talking, Nadia and her father make a commitment to give each other "a lift between switches," to help each other through difficult times.

At Epiphany Middle School, Nadia is in Mrs. Olinski's homeroom. Nadia is extremely quiet and appears to be "cautious about being friendly, about showing [herself]." Julian Singh invites Nadia to Sillington House for tea, and Nadia's life changes forever. She becomes a member of The Souls (she chooses the name of their group) and a member of Mrs. Olinski's Academic Bowl team. Nadia makes wonderful friends and discovers kindness in herself and in others.

Ethan Potter

Ethan is the son of Mr. and Mrs. Potter who are farmers. The Potter family is an established family in Epiphany. Potters have lived "in Clarion County since before Epiphany was a town." Ethan has an older brother named Lucas (nicknamed "Luke"). Luke is the perfect son, athlete, student, and overall citizen. Throughout his life, Ethan has lived in Luke's shadow. He has always felt inferior to Luke, as if he will never be able to measure up. Ethan thinks he is a disappointment to his teachers because he is not the great student Luke was. Ethan feels trapped. His family expects that he will take over the farm one day because "Luke [is] scheduled for greater things." But Ethan doesn't want the farm. He wants to become a set designer or costume designer for the theater. He doesn't tell anyone about this dream; instead, he keeps everything to himself and suffers in silence.

Ethan is extremely quiet and reserved. He is good at watching others and listening. He doesn't talk much. He creates barriers between himself and others to avoid having to participate in relationships. In this way, Ethan believes, other students will never find out that he is not as good as Luke. Ethan is aware that his "silence is a habit that hurts." His silence isolates him and causes him to feel lonely. When Julian Singh begins to take the school bus, Ethan avoids eye contact and conversation with Julian, even though he is curious about Julian. Julian, who is consistently kind and friendly toward Ethan, helps Ethan discover kindness within himself. Ethan's newfound kindness enables him to protect Julian from bullies.

Ethan goes to Sillington House and surprises himself. He finds the courage to tell jokes, ask questions, and be open with Nadia, Noah, and Julian—things he has never done before. Sillington house "made [him] pull sounds out of [his] silence." Ethan gains self-confidence and begins to feel good about himself. He becomes a member of The Souls and Mrs. Olinski's Academic Bowl team.

Julian Singh

Julian is the person responsible for the formation of The Souls and the last person chosen by Mrs. Olinski to be on her academic team. Julian's "skin [is] the color of strong coffee with skim milk" and it has undertones of gray. "His lips are the color of a day-old bruise" and his hair is "blue-black, thick and straight." He has a British accent, carries a leather book bag, and wears shorts and knee socks. Julian has dignity. He is patient, polite, and cheerful even under adverse circumstances. Julian is quite an accomplished magician, who uses his talent wisely. He also has keen senses. He is always aware of Ham, a classmate who teases him, and where he is and what he is doing. Julian is an extremely thoughtful and kind person. Despite Ham's mean plan to bring harm to Ginger, Nadia's dog, Julian does not seek revenge and does not harm Arnold, Froelich's dog, even though he has the opportunity to do so. Julian simply takes the drugged dog treats and later drops them in Ham's lap.

Julian is part East Indian and part American. Throughout his childhood, he attended boarding schools, and during the summers he traveled with his father, a chef, on cruise ships. His mother, who was a singer, is dead. Julian and his father bought the Sillington House and are going to open a Bed and Breakfast inn for guests. The Sillington House is Julian's first stable home. Because he is on a journey to find a place for himself, he invites three classmates—Nadia, Ethan, and Noah—to the Sillington House for tea.

Noah Gershom

Noah is one of The Souls and is chosen by Mrs. Olinski to be on the sixth-grade Academic Bowl team. He is the son of Mrs. Gershom, a realtor, and Dr. Gershom, a dentist. Noah also has a brother named Joey. He knows a lot about myriad subjects; he often recites "facts" and "always [has] an answer for everything." When Julian proposes a project for The Souls, Noah quickly understands that it has to do with helping Mrs. Olinski "stand on [her] own two feet. . . ." Konigsburg implies that it was Noah who suggested The Souls become members of Mrs. Olinski's sixth-grade Academic Bowl team.

Noah's journey begins when he goes to Century Village in Florida to stay with his grandparents, Sadie and Nate Gershom. While he is there, he accidentally becomes the best man at the wedding of Nadia's grandfather and Ethan's grandmother. Noah thinks that he "did a wonderful job" helping with the preparations for the wedding. He is creative, industrious, and resourceful. Noah begins to realize that when he acts out of kindness, others do also. Noah gives up personal items that he has acquired while he has been in Florida, to be used as prizes at the Diamondstein wedding reception. The people who win the prizes end up spreading the kindness to other people. Noah is proud of himself and continues his journey at Sillington House with The Souls and their project to help Mrs. Olinski.

Activities for Readers

1. Using the Internet, research the endangered turtle species mentioned in *The View From Saturday*. What must be done to save the turtles from extinction? What are the chances for the survival of the turtles?

2. When Julian invited Noah, Nadia, and Ethan to tea, the invitations he gives them are very creative and clever. He uses lines from *Alice in Wonderland*. Design four creative and clever invitations that you would give to four people. What theme would you use?

3. Friendship is a significant theme in *The View From Saturday*. Write an acrostic poem about friendship. (An *acrostic* poem is a verse arranged so that it spells words, phrases, or sentences when certain letters are selected in an orderly sequence.)

4. Design a boardgame with questions similar to those asked in the Academic Bowl in the novel. Include the directions for the game as well as playing pieces.

Additional Resources

Children's Literature Review. Vol. 47. Detroit: Gale Research, 1998: 120–154.

Contemporary Authors. Vol. 59. Detroit: Gale Research, 1998: 220–224.

Dowell, Frances. *"The View From Saturday." Dream/Girl Magazine: The Arts Magazine for Girls.* Online. www.dgarts.com/books/a058.htm.

"E.L. Konigsburg." Random House. Online. www.randomhouse.com/teachers/authors/koni.html.

"Interview with E.L. Konigsburg." eToys, Inc. Online. www.etoys.com/html/eb_int_konigsburg.shtml.

Konigsburg, E.L. "Newbery Medal Acceptance Speech." *The Horn Book Magazine.* July–August 1997: 404–414.

"Konigsburg, E.L." *Educational Paperback Association.* Internet. www.edupaperback.org/authorbios/konigsbu.html.

Todd, Laurie Konigsburg. "E.L. Konigsburg." *The Horn Book Magazine.* July–August 1997: 415–417.

THE MIDWIFE'S APPRENTICE (1996)

Life and Background of the Author

A contemporary writer of historical fiction for young adults, Karen Cushman considers herself to be a "late bloomer." At age 53, she wrote her first novel, *Catherine, Called Birdy* (1995), a novel that won numerous awards including a Newbery Honor. Six months later, Cushman finished her second novel, *The Midwife's Apprentice* (1996), and earned the Newbery Medal. Cushman's novels, set in diverse social and historical settings, are about the aristocracy and homeless in medieval England and the California gold rush; however, the struggles faced by her heroines are timeless. Cushman's protagonists are strong females who have a will of their own that surfaces as they discover their identity. Her characters possess hope, determination, and imagination. Cushman writes about universal issues—the search for identity, perseverance, limitations, and the humane treatment of all individuals.

Cushman was born on October 4, 1941, in Chicago, Illinois, to Arthur and Loretta Lipski. Her family moved to Southern California when she was eleven. Cushman discovered the library at an early age, and books became a big part of her life. She loved fiction, but from time to time she would find herself interested in a variety of nonfiction topics such as the Civil War, physiology of the brain, or anesthetics. She read everything she could get her hands on about each topic.

Cushman attended private schools. Because her formal education was not a match for her imagination, she became interested in plays. She would hold plays with friends from her neighborhood. Once, she got a book about ballet and had her friends pretend to be taking a ballet class. Her friends used car door handles like a ballet bar and Cushman read to them, directing them in what to do. One of Cushman's first attempts at writing was a play called *Jingle Bagels*, a multicultural Christmas story in which Santa Claus goes down the wrong chimney and ends up in a Jewish house during Hanukkah. Growing up, she also wrote poems about Elvis Presley and plots for Elvis movies.

After graduating from high school, Cushman won a scholarship and chose to attend Stanford University. She graduated in 1963 with a degree in English and Greek. After graduation, Cushman wanted to go to Greece and dig for treasures in ancient ruins, but instead, she began working for the Beverly Hills telephone company. She eventually quit that job and several subsequent jobs. She was working as an assistant clerk-administrator at Hebrew Union College in Los Angeles, when she met Philip Cushman, then a rabbinical student. They married in 1969 and moved to Oregon. While in Oregon, her husband taught at a small college and Cushman took up weaving and made blackberry jam. They also had a daughter named Leah. Two years later, they returned to California, where Cushman and her husband went back to school to earn master's degrees. Cushman graduated from United States International University in 1977 with a master's in human behavior. Her husband received his master's in counseling. Her husband continued with his studies and received a doctorate in psychology. He has been a psychotherapist and professor ever since. Cushman also continued her studies. She received a second master's in Museum Studies from the John F. Kennedy University in 1986. After graduating, Cushman stayed at John F. Kennedy University, where she has taught classes in museology and material culture, edited the *Museum Studies Journal*, and coordinated the master's project program.

As her daughter, Leah, grew up, Cushman read numerous books to and with her. When Leah began reading adult fiction, Cushman didn't. She chose to keep reading young adult literature because the stories and themes captivated her attention. Cushman began to share her ideas for stories with her husband, until one day he told her to write the stories down.

Because Cushman had always been interested in history, particularly medieval England, she began her research in that area. She read young adult historical novels, including those by Patricia MacLachlan and Rosemary Sutcliff, and attended writers' conferences. She went to Renaissance fairs and listened to medieval music. Despite the fact that many people tried to dissuade Cushman from writing historical fiction, she never gave up. Her first novel, *Catherine, Called Birdy*, was published in 1994 and her second novel, *The Midwife's Apprentice*, was published in 1995. Both stories are set in medieval England. Cushman's research for her novels is extensive. Her goal is to portray the setting of her books as accurately as possible for her readers. All of the old words and expressions in Cushman's books are real, and foods mentioned in the books are from actual cookbooks. Cushman's third book, *The Ballad of Lucy Whipple* (1996), takes place during the California Gold Rush. She is currently at work on a fourth novel.

Both *Catherine, Called Birdy* and *The Midwife's Apprentice* have earned many awards and honors including the Newbery Honor and Newbery Medal (respectively), American Library Association awards, the Notable Children's Book in Language Arts award, Books for Youth Editors' Choice award, Fanfare Honor List award, School Library

Journal's Best Books of the Year award, American Booksellers Association award, and the Gold Kite Award for Fiction from the Society for Children's Book Writers and Illustrators.

Cushman lives in Oakland, California, with her husband, Philip, two cats, a dog, and a rabbit. When she isn't writing, she enjoys working in her garden—growing tomato plants. She also reads and listens to music popular during the Middle Ages. Cushman continues to teach—she is an adjunct professor at John F. Kennedy University in the Museum Studies department—and to write for young adults.

Cushman's Selected Works

Catherine, Called Birdy (1994)

The Midwife's Apprentice (1995)

The Ballad of Lucy Whipple (1996)

A Brief Synopsis

The Midwife's Apprentice is narrated in third person ("she said," as opposed to "I said," which is first person), using a limited omniscient viewpoint (in which only the protagonist's thoughts and feelings are revealed). The novel is set in medieval England.

Character Insight

Brat, the protagonist, or main character of the novel, is a homeless, nameless young girl who might be twelve or thirteen years old (she doesn't know her exact age). Brat has no memory of her parents. For as long as she can remember, she has lived on her own, going from village to village, stealing food or working in exchange for food or a dry place to sleep. One morning, she is discovered sleeping in a warm pile of dung by the village midwife. Brat calls the midwife "Jane Sharp," because she has "a sharp nose and a sharp glance." The midwife calls her "Beetle" and takes her in to work as her servant. In return for her labor, Beetle receives scraps of food and a place to sleep. Even though the midwife is mean to Beetle (slapping Beetle and calling her names), Beetle considers her situation a step up from living on the streets and sleeping in dung. She now has work and a place to live.

Soon, Beetle befriends a stray cat that she rescues from the inhumane treatment of the village boys. Even though she doesn't know how to sing songs or speak gently to the cat, who is close to death, she feels compassion and is relieved when she realizes the cat will live. Beetle begins to give the cat scraps of food she saves from her meager meals and the cat begins to follow her wherever she goes. Later, she names the cat Purr.

Beetle continues to follow the midwife from cottage to cottage, preparing and carrying the midwife's supplies. But Beetle is never allowed to watch the midwife or to learn what the midwife is doing when she helps to deliver a baby. Because she is curious, Beetle watches covertly—looking through cracks in the windows or standing in the shadows of a room out of the midwife's sight. Beetle begins to gain some self-esteem. This becomes evident when she goes to the Saint Swithin's Day Fair for the midwife, to replenish the midwife's supplies. During the course of the day, Beetle is treated with respect. She is complimented, given a comb, and is mistaken for someone who can read. She renames herself "Alyce," and thinks that someone named Alyce *could* be loved.

Back in the village, Alyce is adamant about people calling her "Alyce" and not Beetle. She thinks better of herself and, consequently, acts better. She saves Will, a bully from the village who has always picked on her, from drowning in the river and later helps him deliver twin calves. Alyce finds a homeless boy sleeping in the barn near Will's cow and calves. She feeds him, helps him name himself (giving him a bit of self-respect), and sends him to the manor to find work.

As time passes, the villagers begin to accept Alyce and ask her advice. She earns their respect when she successfully delivers a baby in the midwife's absence. For possibly the first time in her life, Alyce feels pride and smiles. Although Alyce is happy about her accomplishment, the midwife is not. The midwife is angry because she doesn't want competition from Alyce. The midwife is even more upset when a woman in labor asks for Alyce and not for her. When Alyce realizes she can't deliver the baby because it is a difficult birth and she doesn't know what to do, she has to call for the midwife to come to deliver the baby. She is totally humiliated. Feeling like a failure, Alyce takes Purr and runs away.

Theme

Alyce is depressed. She doesn't think she can return to the village. She and Purr arrive at an inn situated at a crossroads. Alyce trades her labor for food and shelter. While working at the inn, Alyce is taught by one of the patrons of the inn to read, and she learns what she wants in her life. What she really wants is to be the midwife's apprentice. A self-respecting Alyce returns to the midwife in the village and asks to be her apprentice once again, vowing never to give up.

Character Map

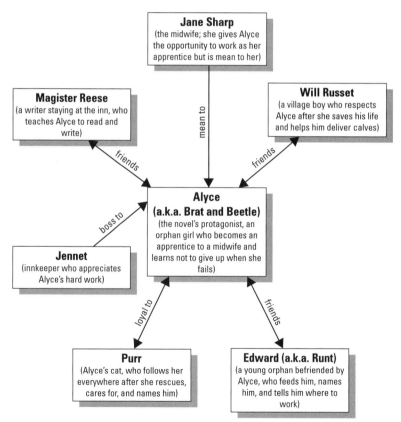

Jane Sharp
(the midwife; she gives Alyce the opportunity to work as her apprentice but is mean to her)

Magister Reese
(a writer staying at the inn, who teaches Alyce to read and write)

Will Russet
(a village boy who respects Alyce after she saves his life and helps him deliver calves)

mean to

friends

friends

**Alyce
(a.k.a. Brat and Beetle)**
(the novel's protagonist, an orphan girl who becomes an apprentice to a midwife and learns not to give up when she fails)

boss to

Jennet
(innkeeper who appreciates Alyce's hard work)

loyal to

friends

Purr
(Alyce's cat, who follows her everywhere after she rescues, cares for, and names him)

Edward (a.k.a. Runt)
(a young orphan befriended by Alyce, who feeds him, names him, and tells him where to work)

Major Themes

In this novel of a young girl's determination to discover a place, or niche, for herself in the world, Cushman has concentrated on two universal themes—the search for identity and a sense of belonging and perseverance in the midst of adversity.

Throughout *The Midwife's Apprentice*, Alyce is on a personal journey to discover who she is and where she belongs. At the start of the novel, Alyce is alone. She has nothing but the clothes on her back. She is mocked and tormented by the bullies in the village. Alyce has no place to go to get away from the bullies and no one to protect her. She is ostracized from "normal" day-to-day activities because she is different—she is homeless and nameless. As Alyce begins to work as the midwife's apprentice, she begins to talk to people and to listen. She realizes that she is not "stupid." She watches the midwife and learns about the uses of herbs. The people in the village begin to respect her opinion and to ask her advice. She learns how to speak in a comforting voice after listening to Will as he delivers calves. She realizes that she is worthy of love when a merchant at the fair tells her so. And, she learns what it feels like to smile and to sing.

Alyce learns what she likes and dislikes, what is important to her and what isn't. For example, she knows that she prefers Will's gentle voice to the midwife's screaming and yelling. Alyce realizes she is not stupid when she learns to read while working at the inn. Alyce really sees herself for the first time after she has taken a bath with soap. She becomes aware of all that she can be and she knows that she can be a good midwife's apprentice. When she returns to the midwife after running away and working at the inn, Alyce is self-confident. She has discovered her identity after much thinking and soul searching. Even though it has not been an easy journey, she now knows who she is, what she wants, and where she belongs.

Cushman's belief in perseverance despite obstacles or challenges that arise throughout life is another major theme. After Alyce is unable to deliver a baby, she gives up and runs away. She tells herself over and over again that she is a failure. Consequently, she truly believes she is a failure, incapable of being the midwife's apprentice. Will shows up at the inn and tells Alyce in a friendly way that she is not a failure, that she can't be expected to know everything. The midwife also visits the inn and comments that she needs an apprentice who doesn't give up.

After successfully delivering a baby at the inn, Alyce gains self-confidence and returns to the village, determined to work as the midwife's apprentice. Cushman reiterates the importance of perseverance as Alyce tells the midwife that, "I know how to try and risk and fail and try again and not give up."

Theme

Cushman exposes readers to the universality of an individual's search for his or her own place in the world, illustrating to her readers that they are not alone in their search. She writes about persevering when faced with life's challenges, showing that everyone falls down, but the people who get up, dust themselves off, and try again are the people who find their niche in the world.

About the Characters

Alyce (previously known as Brat and, later, Beetle)

Alyce is the 12- or 13-year-old (she doesn't know how old she is) protagonist, or main character, of the novel. She is a skinny, pale girl afraid of people and unfamiliar situations and surroundings. Alyce is a dynamic character. She changes during the course of the novel due to her experiences and actions. When the novel begins, Alyce is called Brat. She is homeless. She has no place of her own and she is as poor as anyone can be. She has endured extreme hardships: Her parents abandoned her when she was very young and she has been abused and neglected by people throughout her life (even the midwife kicks her, slaps her, calls her names, and feeds her inadequate amounts of food). She has survived by traveling from village to village, stealing food and working for food or shelter.

Because Alyce has never been rewarded or encouraged, she is unaware that she is a special and unique human being. She experiences feelings of being stupid and unworthy. She is afraid to try anything because she is afraid she will fail. Alyce has no self-confidence. In spite of her low self-esteem and the tormenting and teasing that she tolerates from village bullies, there is an innate goodness about Alyce. In contrast to the midwife, Alyce is compassionate. She adopts a stray cat, names it Purr, and cares for it; she is kind to Will, one of the village bullies; and she gives a homeless boy a name, some food, and tells him where to find work.

When she renames herself "Alyce," her life begins a transformation. She begins to feel a sense of pride and self-respect. After the merchant at the fair gives Alyce a comb and comments on her looks, she peers into a stream and realizes for the first time that she is worthy of love. Alyce begins to tell stories to Purr, sing songs, and smile—things she has never done before. She begins to learn what it feels like to be truly alive.

Alyce, rather than the midwife, is called by a woman in labor to deliver her baby. When she is unable to deliver the baby because it is a complicated birth and has to call for the midwife, she feels like a failure and is ashamed of herself. She runs away with Purr and finds work in an inn not far from the village. There she has time to think and to discover who she really is. Alyce goes to see Edward, the homeless boy she helped, and ends up taking a bath with soap. The bath is a transformation, or rebirth, for Alyce. She emerges a strong girl who knows what she wants to do with her life—and she knows she can do it. She defies her fear and returns to the midwife to become her apprentice once again. Alyce learns to honor herself. She also learns that if she perseveres, she *can* overcome adversity.

Jane, the Midwife

Jane is the only midwife in the village. She assists pregnant women who are in labor by using a combination of herbs, superstition, and common sense. She does her job "with energy and some skill, but without care, compassion, or joy." Jane is a tough and greedy person. She demands high wages for her services because she has no competition—and that is just how she likes it. When she finds Brat in the dung heap, she realizes that she has found cheap labor. She takes Brat—whom she calls Beetle—home with her to work as her servant. Jane is sure that someone who looks as stupid and scared as Beetle will be no competition to her. She allows Beetle to learn about the herbs she uses, but controls Beetle's learning by making her stay outside when she is delivering a baby and by verbally and physically abusing her.

The midwife becomes enraged when a pregnant woman requests Beetle's services and not hers. She accuses Beetle (who is now known as Alyce) of stealing her mothers. The midwife is unaware of the knowledge that Alyce has gleaned from her and she is unaware that the villagers often ask Alyce for advice. Jane doesn't realize how much she depends on Alyce until Alyce runs away.

The midwife goes to the inn where Alyce is working. Speaking to Magister Reese, a guest at the inn, about midwifery, she indirectly tells Alyce that she didn't fail. She tells Magister Reese (knowing full well that Alyce is listening) that she needs an apprentice who will persevere and never give up. In her way, Jane encourages Alyce to be brave. She conveys the message to Alyce that it is better to try and fail—and try again—than to never try at all.

Will Russet

Will is a young red-headed boy who lives in the village. At the beginning of the novel, Will appears to be quite mean. Along with a group of boys, he torments and taunts Beetle every chance he gets. On one occasion, when the boys are drunk, Will falls into the river. Rather than help him, the other boys run off. Alyce (Beetle), who is perched in a tree after running away from the boys, rescues Will. Will thanks her by complimenting her on her bravery. He realizes for the first time that Alyce is a human being with feelings.

As a result of their encounter at the river, Will is reluctant to join the other boys when they harass Alyce. Will again requests Alyce's assistance when his cow is giving birth to calves and can not get out of a pit. Alyce helps Will deliver the calves and Will is grateful to her. He tells people in the village that Alyce brought him luck.

Will, a dynamic character, changes during the course of the novel as a result of his experiences with Alyce. At the conclusion of the novel, when he stops at the Inn with a delivery and sees Alyce, he speaks to her as though she is an old friend. Will has matured and grown up. He sincerely compliments Alyce, tells her she is pretty, and treats her with respect.

Activities for Readers

1. Throughout the novel, the Midwife uses herbal remedies. Using the library or the Internet, research the use of plants for medicines and ailments. Are herbal remedies used today? Make a chart of particular herbs or plants that are used and the ailment they are used for.

2. Choose an incident in the novel that involves Alyce and another character such as Jane, the Midwife, Will, or Edward. Write the scene in first person narrative, from the point of view of the "other" character (Jane, Will, or Edward).

3. Using the library or the Internet, research the Middle Ages. Discover what life was like for young adults living during the thirteenth and fourteenth century.

4. Draw a map of the village and roads leading out of the village. Include landmarks that Cushman mentions in the novel such as the woods and fields, the pond, the castle where Edward goes to live, the Midwife's cottage, and the inn where Alyce goes to work.

Additional Resources

"About the Author: Karen Cushman." Houghton Mifflin Company, 1997. Online. www.eduplace.com/rdg/author/cushman/author bio.html.

"Cushman, Karen." Educational Paperback Association. Online. www.edupaperback.org/authorbios/cushmank.html.

Cushman, Karen. "Newbery Medal Acceptance Speech." *The Horn Book Magazine.* July–August 1996: 413–419.

Cushman, Philip. "Karen Cushman." *The Horn Book Magazine.* July–August 1996: 20–23.

"Karen Cushman." The Internet Public Library. Online. www.ipl.org/youth/AskAuthor/Biographies.html.

Lodge, Sally. "A Talk with Karen Cushman." *Publishers Weekly.* 243 (August 26, 1996): 46.

Rochman, Hazel. "An Interview with Karen Cushman." *Booklist.* 92 (June 1, 1996): 1700–1701.

WALK TWO MOONS (1995)

Life and Background of the Author

Even though Sharon Creech has lived in England and Switzerland since 1979, her main characters are American because that is Creech's "natural narrative voice." To create realistic plots and characters, Creech relies on personal experiences. Her protagonists are sensitive young adults who have a sense of humor in spite of the dilemmas they face throughout adolescence. Creech's novels are usually multilayered and are about topics such as grief, loss, love, and interior journeys. She writes with the intent to expand her readers' horizons; she hopes to increase their awareness and understanding of people who are different from them.

Creech was born on July 29, 1945, in Cleveland, Ohio. She was raised in a Cleveland suburb in the midst of a large, noisy family that gathered around the kitchen table to tell stories. Because the stories were exciting, Creech learned early on to embellish *her* stories and exaggerate, as a guarantee that family members would listen. Throughout elementary school and high school, writing piqued Creech's interest. She attributes her enthusiasm toward writing to her natural inclination to write and to teachers who taught her writing skills and provided encouragement. Creech was fascinated with writing instruments such as pens and pencils, paper, and books. She stockpiled these instruments and treasured them. Creech was also an avid reader. Although she doesn't remember many titles of the books she read, Creech recalls the experience of reading. She loved reading the legends of King Arthur, Greek myths, American Indian myths, and *Ivanhoe* in particular. The most thrilling career she could imagine was that of a writer or a teacher, because teachers use books every day.

After graduating from high school, Creech attended Hiram College, where she received a bachelor's degree, and then George Mason University in Washington, D.C., where she earned a Master of Arts degree. While in graduate school, Creech's interest in writing grew when she took a writing course taught by John Gardner and attended workshops where writers such as John Irving and James Dickey talked about their craft.

During the time Creech was in graduate school, she worked at the Federal Theatre Project Archives and later at the *Congressional Quarterly* as an editorial assistant. She didn't particularly enjoy being an editorial assistant, because the work involved facts and politics, subjects that do not appeal to Creech. For the next several years, Creech remained in Washington, D.C. She was married, had two children, Rob and Karin, and was divorced. In 1979, Creech got a job teaching literature at an American school located in a Surrey village in England. She and her children packed up and moved. In 1981, Creech married Lyle D. Rigg, the assistant headmaster (assistant principal) at the school in England where Creech was teaching. Like Creech, Rigg was originally from Ohio. Soon after getting married, Rigg was transferred to The American School in Switzerland (TASIS) in Lugano, Switzerland. Rigg, Creech, and Creech's two children lived in Lugano for two years. In 1984, the family returned to the TASIS in England where Creech teaches American and British literature and her husband is headmaster.

Creech concentrated on her family and her teaching for many years. It wasn't until her father had a stroke and was unable to speak that Creech began writing her first novel. She was fearful that her words would be locked inside her forever, as they had been for her father during the six long years before his death. Creech's first two books, *The Recital* (1990) and *Nickel Malley* (1991), were published in England for adults under the name Sharon Rigg. Her first novel for young adults, *Absolutely Normal Chaos*, published in 1991 also in England, is a book about a large, rowdy family like her own. *Walk Two Moons* was published in the United States in 1994, earning Creech the Newbery Medal Award in 1995, the *School Library Journal* Best Books Award (1994), the Notable Children's Books Award (1995), and the Young Reader's Award (1997).

Creech maintains a loose connection between her novels. The fictional town of Bybanks, Kentucky, on the Ohio River plays a part in the life of almost all of her protagonists. Often a character mentioned in one novel will surface in another novel. For example, Mary Lou Finney who is a minor character in *Walk Two Moons* (1994) is the main character of *Absolutely Normal Chaos* (1990).

Along with writing novels, Creech has published poetry and short stories. She has also written a play that was produced in New York City in 1992 entitled *The Center of the Universe: Waiting for the Girl.*

Today, Creech continues to write novels for adolescents and to teach and live in England with her husband. Creech and her husband live in England during the school term; during the summer months, they live in Chautauqua Lake, New York. Creech enjoys seeing her children, who both live in the United States, and spending time exploring her home country.

Creech's Selected Works

Absolutely Normal Chaos (1991)

Walk Two Moons (1994)

Pleasing the Ghost (1996)

Chasing Redbird (1997)

Bloomability (1998)

The Wanderer (2000)

Fishing in the Air (2000)

A Brief Synopsis

Style & Language

Creech wrote *Walk Two Moons* in the first person, revealing the thoughts and feelings of the protagonist, Salamanca Tree Hiddle (Sal), a young girl searching for her mother. The novel is a story-within-a-story. Creech writes about Sal's road trip to Idaho with her eccentric grandparents, and during the trip, Sal tells her grandparents about her friend Phoebe Winterbottom and the disappearance of Phoebe's mother. In the telling of her story, the tragic events of her own mother's disappearance and parallels between the situations and reactions of the girls are revealed.

Character Insight

Sal lived on a farm in Bybanks, Kentucky, with her mother and father. Her parents seemed to love each other very much and Sal, "a country girl at heart," was at home on the farm. Sal's mother has a still-born baby and, afterward, becomes quite depressed. She can't seem to work through her grief. Her solution is to go away "to clear her head, and to clear her heart of all the bad things." Sal and her father try to persuade her not to go, but she leaves anyway. Sal and her father are lost without her mother, but eventually they settle into a routine of their own. Sal is angry at her mother for leaving. Her mother sends her postcards from every stop the bus makes en route to Idaho. One day, Sal's father learns that her mother won't be coming home. Sal's mother is killed in a bus accident. Her father goes to Idaho to bury Sal's mother.

Theme

Not long after Sal's father returns from Idaho, he decides to sell the farm. He can't stay there because memories of Sal's mother are everywhere. Sal can't bear the thought of selling the farm. She cannot let go of the memories of her mother and, because she has no closure on her mother's death, such as a funeral, she continues to hope that one day her mother will come home. Sal is angry and she is in denial about her mother's death. Her father rents the farm instead of selling it, and the two of them move to Euclid, Ohio where Margaret Cadaver, a new friend of her father's, lives. They rent a small house a few blocks from Margaret's. Sal's father met Margaret when he went to Idaho. Margaret, the only survivor of the crash, had been sitting next to Sal's mother on the bus.

Literary Device

Sal hates the new house and she doesn't want to have anything to do with Margaret. She is sad and angry, and she misses her mother terribly. She also feels guilty. She feels it is her fault her mother left in the first place. Sal meets Phoebe Winterbottom, who lives across the street from Margaret. Phoebe is in Sal's class at school and the two girls become friends. They spend time at each other's house and both of them visit Mary Lou Finney from time to time. Mary Lou has a cousin named Ben who is living with her family. He is also in Sal's class, and Sal and Ben become more than friends—they fall in love.

Character Insight

Sal begins to realize that Phoebe's mother seems unhappy. She is not surprised when Phoebe goes home from school one day and finds that her mother has disappeared. Mrs. Winterbottom has left Phoebe, her sister, and Mr. Winterbottom notes and has stocked the freezer with food. Phoebe is angry and hurt because her mother has abandoned her. Phoebe acts like an "ornery donkey." Sal realizes this is the way she must have acted when her mother left her. Eventually, Phoebe's mother does return to the house with a young man who, she tells the family, is a son she had put up for adoption before she married Mr. Winterbottom. Creech leads readers to believe that Mrs. Winterbottom will be staying home and that major changes will take place in the Winterbottom household.

At the same time Mrs. Winterbottom leaves, anonymous messages are left on the Winterbottom's front porch. Phoebe is convinced a "lunatic" has left the messages. Sal and Phoebe spend time investigating the disappearance of Phoebe's mother and the mystery messages. Phoebe believes the "lunatic" is a young man who came to the door one day—the young man turns out to be her half brother, and the "lunatic" who was leaving the messages, turns out to be Mrs. Partridge, Margaret's blind mother.

After everything is more or less settled with Phoebe's family, Sal's grandparents, Gram and Gramps Hiddle, suggest they take a road trip from Ohio to Idaho to see Sal's mother's grave. They take the same route that Sal's mother took when she left home on the bus. Throughout the trip, Sal tells her grandparents about Phoebe, the disappearance of Phoebe's mother, the "lunatic," and Sal's budding romance with Ben.

Theme

Sal and her grandparents travel through Indiana, Illinois, Wisconsin, Minnesota, South Dakota, Wyoming, and finally Idaho. In Illinois they stop and put their feet in Lake Michigan. Sal understands that when Gram says, "Huzza, huzza!" she is expressing joy. Her grandmother dances with Indians in Wisconsin and gets bitten by a poisonous snake in South Dakota, forcing her to spend the night in the hospital. They see Mount Rushmore and Old Faithful. By the time they get to Coeur D'Alene, Idaho, Gram is not feeling well. They drive directly to the hospital and Gram is admitted. The doctors tell Sal and Gramps that Gram has had a stroke; Gram dies early the next morning. Sal is not at the hospital when Gram dies, because she drove Gramps' car to Lewiston to see the site of her mother's accident. She then spends time in the cemetery at her mother's grave, in an attempt to memorize every detail. Sal is able to put closure on her mother's abandonment of her and can accept her mother's death. She realizes that the trip to Idaho "had been a gift from Gram and Gramps to [her]. They were giving [her] a chance to walk in [her] mother's moccasins—to see what she had seen and feel what she might have felt on her last trip."

Sal and her father return to the farm in Bybanks, Kentucky to live. Gramps is living with them and Gram is buried in the Aspen grove. Gramps has a new beagle puppy named Huzza Huzza. Sal misses her mother, but she is happy being back on the farm she loves so much.

Character Map

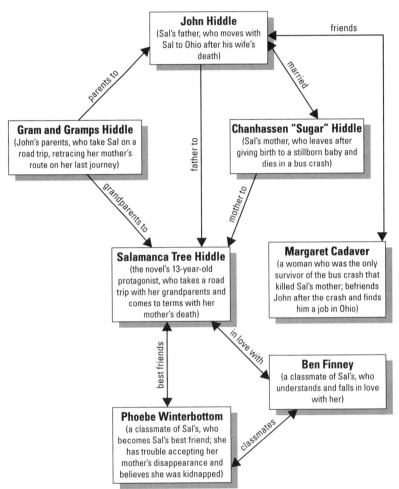

John Hiddle
(Sal's father, who moves with Sal to Ohio after his wife's death)

friends

parents to

married

Gram and Gramps Hiddle
(John's parents, who take Sal on a road trip, retracing her mother's route on her last journey)

father to

Chanhassen "Sugar" Hiddle
(Sal's mother, who leaves after giving birth to a stillborn baby and dies in a bus crash)

grandparents to

mother to

Salamanca Tree Hiddle
(the novel's 13-year-old protagonist, who takes a road trip with her grandparents and comes to terms with her mother's death)

Margaret Cadaver
(a woman who was the only survivor of the bus crash that killed Sal's mother; befriends John after the crash and finds him a job in Ohio)

in love with

best friends

Ben Finney
(a classmate of Sal's, who understands and falls in love with her)

Phoebe Winterbottom
(a classmate of Sal's, who becomes Sal's best friend; she has trouble accepting her mother's disappearance and believes she was kidnapped)

classmates

Major Themes

The major themes of *Walk Two Moons* include the feelings of grief as a response to death and loss, the discovery of self-identity, and hope. Creech uses Sal's physical journey to Idaho with her grandparents and the story she tells about Phoebe Winterbottom to portray her thematic messages.

As Sal tells about the disappearance of Phoebe's mother, and Phoebe's reaction to her loss, she recognizes similarities in her own experience when her mother deserts her (and her father) and is later killed in an accident. Both girls experience the stages of grief: anger, denial, and acceptance. Sal's initial thoughts, like Phoebe's, are "How could she do that? How could she leave me?" Sal is numb and cannot identify her feelings. When Sal's father tells her they are moving to Euclid, Sal throws "colossal temper tantrums." She remembers being ornery, just like Phoebe. Sal doesn't want to leave the farm, because she feels her mother might return. Likewise, Phoebe doesn't want to leave her house because her mother might call. Sal and Phoebe are both in denial about their mother's desertion. When Sal tells her father that Phoebe's mother has disappeared, he comforts her by saying "people usually come back." Despite the fact that her father is speaking generally, Sal finds hope in her father's comment. She believes that maybe her mother will come home and everything will be the way it used to be. Even when Mr. Winterbottom shows Phoebe all the food her mother left in the freezer in preparation for her departure, Phoebe still doesn't want to admit that her mother has left them. Sal and Phoebe both desperately want to believe their mother will be coming home. Because Sal is not able to see her dead mother or attend her funeral, she cannot put closure on her mother's life. It is not until Sal actually sees the accident site, sits at her mother's grave, and reads the headstone that she can finally accept her mother's death. Creech presents the notion that death and loss, as well as grief, are universal. All human beings experience the pain of loss. Creech allows her characters to experience the pain of loss as well as the feelings that accompany the acceptance of loss.

Another significant theme of the novel is the inner journey that every adolescent embarks upon as he or she gains independence from parents and gains self-identity. As Sal takes a physical journey across the United States with her grandparents, she also takes an inner journey that causes her to change. Before she leaves on her road trip, Sal still believes her mother will return one day.

After her mother leaves, Sal doesn't know how to feel. She had always been a mirror of her mother—"if [her mother] was happy, [she] was happy. If [her mother] was sad, [Sal] was sad." She sees a calf and feels happy. She realizes for the first time in her life that she has feelings of her own without her mother's presence. Sal believes her mother might have left to set Sal free. She feels independence from her mother. By telling Phoebe's story, Sal learns that she had nothing to do with her mother leaving because her mother chose to leave. Sal is able to let go of the guilt she has been feeling ever since her mother left. Sal also understands, for the first time, the magnitude of her father's grief. She is able to forgive her father for not taking her with him when he went to Idaho to bury her mother. As a consequence of taking an inner journey, Creech suggests that individuals gain insight that leads to maturity and independence.

Creech also includes the theme of hope for readers. Sal's Indian heritage is important to her because she needs stories of reincarnation to give her hope for the future. Creech also includes Pandora's box as a source of hope. Sal looks into Pandora's box and sees the horrible things that are a part of the world. She also sees that "most people seem a lot like us: sometimes afraid and sometimes brave, sometimes cruel and sometimes kind." Sal chooses to hold on to the hope that is in the bottom of Pandora's box and turn "to the other box, the one with the smooth beautiful folds inside." Creech believes that in order to be brave enough to face the evils in the world, everyone needs hope.

Other themes that Creech includes in *Walk Two Moons* are love for others, such as the love Gram and Gramps have for each other, the love that was evident between Sal's parents, the love that is present in the Finney household, and the love that develops between Sal and Ben. Separation from others and growing apart, both as a natural part of growing up and unexpected or forced separations, and the importance of not judging another man "until you've walked two moons in his moccasins" are also significant themes.

About the Characters

Salamanca Tree Hiddle (Sal)

Sal was brought up on a farm in Bybanks, Kentucky. She is 13 years old and is a "country girl at heart." Like her mother, she has long black hair and is proud of her Seneca Indian heritage. Her parents tried to name her after the name of the Indian tribe to which her great-great-grandmother belonged, but they made a mistake. They named her Salamanca instead of Seneca. And because her mother thought trees were beautiful, Tree became her middle name. Trees play an important role in Sal's life. She prays to trees (because there is always a tree close by), and she has a "singing" tree on the farm.

Sal's inner journey through the grieving process is evident throughout the novel. She denies that her mother is dead. She insists that her mother will be coming home again. She longs for everything to be the way it was. Sal is angry and, at times, she is "ornery and stubborn as an old donkey." She wants someone to blame for her mother's abandonment of her, but her father is too good and her mother is a part of her.

Sal takes a road trip with her grandparents. She wants to see her mother's grave, but is afraid at the same time. At first Sal wants to rush to get to Lewiston, Idaho, because she feels she has to be there in time for her mother's birthday, but as they do get closer, she wants to slow down because she is scared. When Sal finally sees her mother's grave and headstone with a tree engraved on it, she knows once and for all that her mother will never be coming home.

Sal does not think she is brave. She is scared of "lots and lots of things." Sometimes she pretends to be brave when that is what people expect of her, even if she is scared to death. After her mother leaves her, Sal is afraid other people she cares about will leave also. Consequently, Sal doesn't trust people easily. She learns to trust Ben over time and eventually falls in love with him.

Sal also learns to trust Phoebe. They become close friends. Sal is attracted to Phoebe "like a magnet." Sal sees Phoebe as another version of herself—the only difference is that Phoebe acts out the way Sal sometimes feels.

Sal and her father move back to their farm and Gramps moves in with them. Sal misses her mother and is jealous of the fact that Phoebe's mother came back and her mother didn't, but Sal is no longer angry. She is content with her life as it is on the farm.

Phoebe Winterbottom

Phoebe is 13 years old. She lives with her parents and older sister, Prudence, next door to Margaret Cadaver in Euclid, Ohio. Phoebe has a round face, curly blonde hair, and large, sky-blue eyes. She is quiet and keeps to herself most of the time. Phoebe's family is a lot like the Pickfords, Sal's mother's family. They are polite and formal with each other. They rarely laugh and play together. Phoebe loves her father and thinks he is perfect. Even though Phoebe complains about her family, she defends them to anyone who dares to make a critical comment.

When Phoebe's mother disappears, Phoebe is in denial about her mother's abandonment. She refuses to believe her mother would just leave her. She has a "powerful imagination" and comes to the conclusion that the "lunatic" who has been leaving notes at their door must have kidnapped her mother. Phoebe is also a "champion worrier." She thinks someone is watching the house, she hears noises, and she is suspicious of everyone. People are not ordinary to Phoebe; "they are either perfect (like her father) . . . or they are lunatics. . . ."

Phoebe befriends Sal and, together, they investigate the "kidnapping" of Phoebe's mother. Because Phoebe is quite dramatic, she collects hair samples from her house and takes them to the police station, insisting they investigate the kidnapping of her mother.

Underneath Phoebe's annoying comments (she sometimes sounds like a grown-up) and ornery disposition, she is frightened that her mother is not going to come home. When her mother finally comes back, with her illegitimate son, Phoebe expresses her anger toward her mother. She is confused because her life will never be the same.

John Hiddle

John is Sal's father. He is a "kind, honest, simple, and good man . . . he likes plain and simple things . . . his favorite clothes are the flannel shirts and blue jeans that he has had for twenty years." He has had the same car for fifteen years. John is a considerate, sensitive man. He does things like shovel his parents' driveway when it snows, he buys small, thoughtful gifts for his wife and daughter, and he never seems to get angry. John loves working on the farm because he can be outside and can work with the land and animals.

When his wife, Sugar, leaves, John is devastated. He fumbles around until he and Sal finally fall into a routine of their own—and then he finds out that his wife has been killed in a bus accident. He goes to Idaho to bury his wife. John deals with his grief by spending "three days chipping away at the fireplace hidden behind the plaster wall." He replaces bricks and writes Sugar's real name, Chanhassen, in the cement. Finally, John can't stand being at the farm any longer. He sees Sugar everywhere; his memories and sadness are overwhelming. He loved Sugar very much.

John and Sal move to Euclid, Ohio. Margaret Cadaver helps John get a job selling farm machinery. He spends time with Margaret because she is his connection to his dead wife. John is grieving, and he understands that Sal is grieving also. He pays attention to Sal and hugs her, talks to her, comforts her, and gives her the space and time she needs to grieve for her mother. When they are ready, and can accept the fact that Sugar is never going to come home, John and Sal return to the farm.

Chanhassen "Sugar" Hiddle

Chanhassen was Sal's mother. Chanhassen is an Indian name that means "tree sweet juice," or maple sugar. Hence, her nickname "Sugar." Sugar had long black hair, was a physically strong woman, and was not afraid of hard work. She enjoyed living on the farm because she could be close to nature and she could be outdoors. She attributed her love of nature to her Indian heritage. Her great-grandmother was a Seneca Indian and Sugar was proud of her Indian heritage.

Sugar's parents are the Pickfords. They are prim and proper people who never laugh. They are too "busy being respectable" to have fun or enjoy life. They are extremely conservative and stiff; they stand straight up and wear starched clothes. Because Sugar grew up in the Pickford household, the environment had an affect on her. She has low self-esteem and always feels as though she is not good enough. She compares herself to her husband and his happy-go-lucky family, and she feels inferior.

Sugar becomes quite depressed when her baby is stillborn. She is grieving and can't stop the feelings she is experiencing. Her solution is to go away. She wants to go to Lewiston, Idaho, to visit a cousin she hadn't seen in fifteen years. Sugar thinks her cousin will be able to tell her "what [she] is really like . . . before [she] became a wife and mother." Sugar doesn't feel brave or good. She wants to "learn about what she was."

Sugar leaves Sal a letter explaining her departure and takes a bus to Lewiston, Idaho. She sends postcards to Sal along the way telling her that she loves Sal and misses her. Then, the bus has an accident in Lewiston, Idaho, and Sugar is killed.

Gram and Gramps Hiddle

Gram and Gramps are Sal's father's parents from Kentucky. They do not live far from their son's farm. Their language is sprinkled with colorful expressions and slang such as "chickabiddy" and "gooseberry." Gramps has a raspy voice and is curious about everything, and Gram has a whispery voice and expresses spontaneous moments of joy by saying "Huzza, huzza!" Gram and Gramps are "full up to the tops of their heads with goodness and sweetness, and mixed in with all that goodness and sweetness [is] a large dash of peculiarity . . . you could never predict what they would do or say."

Gram and Gramps take Sal on a road trip to Lewiston, Idaho. They give her the opportunity to "walk in [her] mother's moccasins." They follow the same route her mother took on the bus and stop at some of the places her mother stopped. The close, loving relationship that exists between Gram and Gramps is evident during the trip. They know each other well, and treat each other with kindness and respect. They live in the moment and are excited about life.

After Gram dies in Coeur d'Alene, Idaho, Gramps has her body flown back to Kentucky. He buries her in the aspen grove on the farm. Gramps moves to the farm and lives with his son and granddaughter, Sal.

Ben Finney

Ben is Mary Lou Finney's cousin. He is living with the Finney's temporarily. He has large black eyes and black eyelashes. Ben is in Sal's class at school. He draws cartoons as a means of expressing himself. Ben likes Sal. He watches her and, from time to time, he tries to kiss her. He is perceptive, noticing that every time he touches Sal, she jumps. Ben seems to understand Sal. In English class, the students have to spontaneously draw a picture of their souls. Ben's picture is identical to Sal's.

Like Sal, Ben is suffering. Sal's mother abandoned her by leaving and then dying. Ben's mother abandoned him by being sick and needing to be in a mental hospital. Ben is lonely. He visits his mother even though she doesn't seem to be aware of his presence. Ben has a connection to Sal and falls in love with her.

Margaret Cadaver

Margaret lives in a small house in Euclid, Ohio. She has wild red hair and gray eyes. Her mother, who lives with her, is Mrs. Partridge. Margaret's brother is Mr. Birkway, Sal's English teacher. Margaret is a nurse. Her husband was killed and her mother lost her sight when a drunk driver hit Margaret's husband's car.

Margaret was sitting next to Sugar on the bus when the accident happened in Lewiston, Idaho. Margaret was the only survivor of the crash. She met John Hiddle, Sal's father, when John went to Lewiston to bury his wife. They became friends and corresponded with each other. She helps John Hiddle find a job in Euclid and spends time with him. She is friendly towards Sal, but she is not pushy. She is patient with Sal when Sal acts ornery toward her, and when Sal is ready to listen, Margaret explains her connection to Sal's father.

Activities for Readers

1. Write a book review of *Walk Two Moons* similar to book reviews seen in a major newspaper in your area.

2. Draw a map of the United States and trace the route that Sal and her grandparents took from Ohio to Lewiston, Idaho. Identify points of interest and cities where Sal and her grandparents stopped to spend the night, sightsee, or eat.

3. Creech's book, *Absolutely Normal Chaos*, is about Mary Lou Finney, a minor character in *Walk Two Moons*. Choose a minor character from the novel such as Ben, Tom Fleet, Margaret Cadaver, or Mr. Birkwell and write a short story about the character.

4. Creech writes about the intergenerational bonding that takes place between Sal and her grandparents. She also writes about Sal's grandparents on her mother's side and the influences of each set of grandparents on her parents and on her. Draw a family tree tracing your family as far back as you can. How have your ancestors influenced you and your parents?

Additional Resources

Children's Literature Review. Vol. 42. Detroit: Gale Research, 1997: 36–44.

Cooper, Ilene. "*Walk Two Moons.*" *Booklist.* 91 (November 15, 1994): 590.

Creech, Sharon. "Newbery Medal Acceptance Speech." *The Horn Book Magazine.* July–August 1995: 418–425.

Rigg, Lyle D. "Sharon Creech." *The Horn Book Magazine.* July–August 1995: 426–429.

Saville, Alex. "Walking in Their Shoes." February 1, 2000. Princeton Packet Online. Internet. www.pacpub.com/new/enter/2-1-00/creech.html.

"Sharon Creech." *Achuka.* Internet. www.achuka.co.uk/scint.htm.

"Sharon Creech." *Educational Paperback Association.* Internet. www.edupaperback.org/authorbios/creechsh.html.

THE GIVER (1994)

Life and Background of the Author

Lois Lowry is a prolific writer. Since her first book, *A Summer to Die*, was published in 1977, she has written over twenty novels for young adults and has won numerous awards. Her writing style varies from the lighthearted, humorous Anastasia books to the much more serious issues (evident in Lowry's two Newbery Medal winners, *Number the Stars* and *The Giver*) that are a part of the adult world young people are preparing to enter. Her books portray sensitive, intelligent, witty protagonists faced with challenges and choices. Lowry writes about life transitions, the importance of family, true friendship, and the need for caring relationships between all human beings despite their differences.

Lowry was born in Honolulu, Hawaii, on March 20, 1937, to Robert E. Hammersberg, a United States Army dentist, and Katherine Landis Hammersberg. Because her father was a career Army officer, Lowry often moved during her childhood. Leaving Hawaii, her family moved to New York, and, in 1942 Lowry began kindergarten in a private school. She remembers wearing dog tags (identification tags) on a gold chain around her neck that were similar to the dog tags worn by her father. When her father was sent overseas, where he was stationed during most of World War II, her mother took Lowry and her older sister, Helen, to Pennsylvania to live with her family. During this time in Pennsylvania, Lowry's grandfather showered her with attention and affection, but her step-grandmother merely tolerated her. Because Lowry was a shy, introverted child, she sought companionship and entertainment in the wonderful worlds that existed within the books she found in her grandfather's library. While Lowry's father was overseas, her mother had a baby boy, named Jon, whom Lowry loved having in the house. After the war, Lowry and her family joined her father in Tokyo, Japan, where they lived for two years in an Americanized community.

At the outbreak of the Korean War in 1950, Lowry returned to the United States to attend a small, private high school in New York City. She had just turned 17 years old when she graduated from high school in a class of close to fifty students. The caption under her senior picture in the school yearbook reads, "Future Novelist." The following fall, Lowry entered Pembroke College, a branch of Brown University, in Rhode Island, to pursue her childhood dream of becoming a writer. However, she dropped out at the end of her sophomore year to get married at the age of 19. Because her husband, Donald Lowry, was a Naval officer, Lowry resumed a military lifestyle that included traveling and living wherever her husband was stationed. When her husband left the service to attend Harvard Law School, they settled in Cambridge, Massachusetts. After her husband finished law school, the Lowry family, which now included four children, moved to Portland, Maine. Lowry eventually received a bachelor's degree in 1973, at the age of 36, from the University of Southern Maine, and then immediately began work on a master's degree.

While attending graduate school, Lowry established herself as an accomplished freelance journalist. She began writing stories and articles that appeared in publications such as *Redbook*, *Yankee*, and *Down East*, as well as in newspapers. She also edited two textbooks—*Black American Literature* (1973) and *Literature of the American Revolution* (1974), both written by J. Weston Walsh—and became a photographer, specializing in photographs of children. In 1978, a collection of her photographs of buildings and houses was published in a book titled *Here in Kennebunkport*.

Lowry's first novel, *A Summer to Die* (1977), is about the relationship between two adolescent sisters, Meg and Molly, and the effect that Molly's death, as a result of leukemia, has on the family. Lowry based the relationship between Meg and Molly on her own memories of her relationship with her older sister, Helen, as they were growing up, and on the feelings and emotions that she felt when Helen died at the age of twenty-eight of cancer. Lowry experienced other heartaches as well. Lowry's oldest son, Grey, a fighter pilot in the United States Air Force, was killed in a plane crash in 1995. In addition, Lowry has a daughter who became disabled as a result of a disease involving the central nervous system. Her daughter's disability has reinforced Lowry's belief that people are "connected" despite their physical differences.

In 1977, Lowry and her husband divorced, and Lowry remained in Maine for the next two years, continuing to write. After completing another serious novel, *Find a Stranger, Say Goodbye* (1978), Lowry moved to Boston. Because she had been writing about serious and sad issues, she decided to write a humorous short story about a 10-year-old girl named Anastasia Krupnik. Anastasia is a gangly girl who wears glasses, has messy blonde hair, and is always getting into mischief. Lowry liked Anastasia and her family so much that the short story became the first chapter of her novel *Anastasia Krupnik* (1979), the first in a series of novels about Anastasia.

Lowry lives in Cambridge, Massachusetts and spends most weekends at her nineteenth-century farmhouse in New Hampshire. She spends at least five hours writing every single morning, working on more than one project at a time. When she isn't writing, she likes to cook, garden in the summer, and knit in the winter. She enjoys reading memoirs and biographies, taking exotic, adventurous trips, and going to as many movies as possible. She is also an accomplished photographer. The photograph of a young Swedish girl on the cover of the Yearling-Newbery edition of *Number the Stars* was taken by Lowry.

Lowry's novels cover a variety of topics that range in tone from serious to humorous and share many of the same themes: freedom, friendship, and the interdependency that exists between people. Through her writing, Lowry communicates her hope for human decency to exist in the world.

Lowry's Selected Works

Novels

A Summer to Die (1977)

Find a Stranger, Say Goodbye (1978)

Here in Kennebunkport (1978)

Anastasia Krupnik (1979)

Autumn Street (1980)

Anastasia Again! (1981)

Anastasia at Your Service (1982)

The One Hundredth Thing About Caroline (1983)

Taking Care of Terrific (1983)

Us and Uncle Fraud (1984)

Anastasia, Ask Your Analyst (1984)

Switcharound (1985)

Anastasia on Her Own (1985)

Anastasia Has the Answers (1986)

Rabble Starkey (1987)

Anastasia's Chosen Career (1987)

All About Sam (1988)

Number the Stars (1989)

Your Move, J.P.! (1990)

Anastasia at This Address (1991)

Attaboy, Sam! (1992)

The Giver (1993)

Anastasia, Absolutely (1995)

See You Around, Sam! (1996)

Stay! Keeper's Story (1997)

Looking Back: A Book of Memories (1998)

Zooman Sam (1999)

Gathering Blue (2000)

Short Stories

"Crow Call." (*Redbook*. December 1975)

"Splendor," *Short Takes: A Short Story Collection for Young Readers*. (Elizabeth Segal, editor, 1986)

"The Harringtons' Daughter," *A Gathering of Flowers: Stories about Being Young in America*. (Joyce Carol Thomas, editor, 1990)

"The Tree House," *The Big Book for Peace*. (Ann Durrell and Marily Sachs, editors, 1990)

"Elliot's House," *The Big Book for Our Planet*. (Ann Durrell, Jean Craighead George, and Katherine Paterson, editors, 1993)

"Holding," *Am I Blue?: Coming Out from the Silence*. (Marion Dane Bauer, editor, 1994)

A Brief Synopsis

Literary
Device

Lowry narrates *The Giver* in third person, using a limited omniscient viewpoint (only Jonas' thoughts and feelings are revealed). Through Jonas' eyes, his community appears to be a utopia—a perfect place—that is self-contained and isolated from Elsewhere, every other place in the world. No evidence of disease, hunger, poverty, war, or lasting pain exists in the community. Jonas' family, like all other families in the community, includes a caring mother and father and two children—one male child and one female child. Jonas' mother has an important job with the Department of Justice, and his father has a job as a Nurturer, taking care of newborns. Jonas has one younger sister, Lily. His family *seems* ideal. Each morning, they discuss their dreams from the previous night; during the evening meal, they share feelings about the events of the day, comforting and supporting each other according to the rules of the community.

As we learn more about Jonas' family, we also learn about the community as a whole. Family units must apply for children; spouses do not get to choose one another but, instead, are matched; and grandparents do not exist. All of a sudden, this utopia that Lowry has created doesn't seem quite right. The mood is foreboding, a feeling that something bad will happen and suggesting that Jonas' community is far from perfect.

A long time ago, the people in Jonas' community chose to have the community ruled by a Committee of Elders. The Committee of Elders controls everyone and everything, blasting rules and reprimands from loudspeakers located throughout the community, including in every family dwelling. A total of fifty infants are born to Birthmothers every year. Each peer group is identified by its age—for example, Threes, Sevens, Nines—and must follow specific rules about appropriate clothing, haircuts, and activities for that particular peer group. When children become Eights, they begin mandatory volunteering and are closely observed by the Committee of Elders so that the committee can assign a lifelong profession to each child at the Ceremony of Twelve, which takes place every year during the December Ceremony.

Literary Device

The Giver begins with Jonas' apprehension about his Ceremony of Twelve, when he will be assigned his lifelong job. He can guess which jobs his friends, Fiona and Asher, will be assigned, but he has no idea what his own job Assignment will be. At the Ceremony, Jonas learns that he has been selected to become the next Receiver of Memory, the highest position in the community.

Theme

Jonas begins training under the present Receiver of Memory, an older man whom Jonas calls The Giver. The Giver lives alone in private rooms that are lined with shelves full of books. Jonas' training involves receiving, from The Giver, all of the emotions and memories of experiences that the people in the community chose to give up to attain Sameness and the illusion of social order. The first memory that Jonas receives from The Giver is a sled ride down a snow-covered hill.

Jonas has never before experienced going downhill, cold weather, or snow. Eventually, through memories, The Giver teaches Jonas about color, love, war, and pain. Jonas begins to understand the hypocrisy that exists in his community—that is, the illusion that everything in the community is good when, in fact, it isn't. The people *appear* to love each other, but they don't really know what love feels like because their lives are a charade; their reactions have been trained. Jonas realizes that people have given up their freedoms to feel and think as individuals, choosing instead to be controlled by others.

Character Insight

One day, Jonas asks The Giver if he can watch a video of a release his father performed on an infant earlier that morning. He watches and is horrified when he realizes that a release is really forced death by lethal injection. Jonas discusses his feelings with The Giver, and they decide on a plan that will force the people to give up Sameness. However, before they can carry out their plan, Jonas learns that Gabriel, a 2-year-old infant who has been staying with Jonas' family unit because Gabriel has trouble sleeping through the night, is going to be released—killed. To prevent Gabriel from being killed, Jonas takes Gabriel, whom he loves, and together they ride a bicycle out of the community. Because Jonas leaves the community, all of the memories that Jonas has received from The Giver will be transmitted back to the citizens in the community, forcing them to experience feelings and emotions and to remember their past. His hope, and The Giver's hope, is that when Jonas leaves and the community must face the memories, they will change their way of life and let feeling and emotion back in.

Literary Device

Jonas travels for days and days with Gabriel, who is dying from starvation and the cold weather. Finally, they come to the top of a hill where there is snow and a sled. They get on the sled and ride downhill toward music and Christmas lights. What actually happens to Jonas and Gabriel? Do they die? Are they dreaming? Do they go to a house with lights and music? Do they end up back in their original community? Do the people in the community change? All of these questions are left unanswered at the end of the book. Lowry intentionally writes an ambiguous ending so that readers can decide for themselves what happens to Jonas and Gabriel at the end of *The Giver*.

Character Map

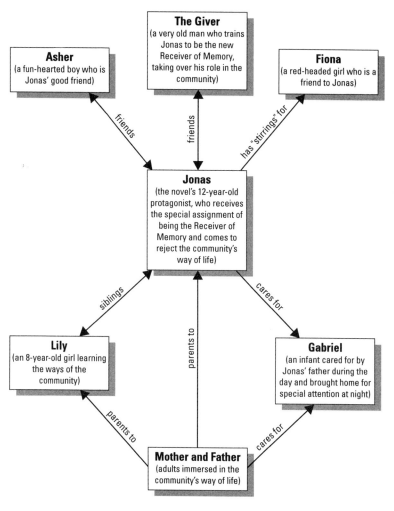

The Giver
(a very old man who trains Jonas to be the new Receiver of Memory, taking over his role in the community)

Asher
(a fun-hearted boy who is Jonas' good friend)

Fiona
(a red-headed girl who is a friend to Jonas)

friends

friends

has "stirrings" for

Jonas
(the novel's 12-year-old protagonist, who receives the special assignment of being the Receiver of Memory and comes to reject the community's way of life)

siblings

parents to

cares for

Lily
(an 8-year-old girl learning the ways of the community)

Gabriel
(an infant cared for by Jonas' father during the day and brought home for special attention at night)

parents to

cares for

Mother and Father
(adults immersed in the community's way of life)

Geography

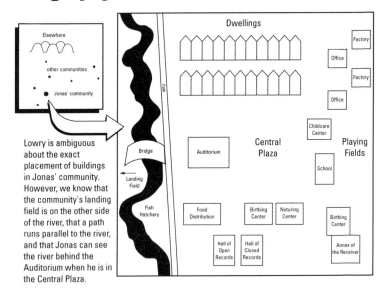

Lowry is ambiguous about the exact placement of buildings in Jonas' community. However, we know that the community's landing field is on the other side of the river, that a path runs parallel to the river, and that Jonas can see the river behind the Auditorium when he is in the Central Plaza.

Major Themes

Many themes in *The Giver* demonstrate Lowry's concerns about society and humanity. For example, she concentrates on the tradeoffs involved when Jonas' community chooses Sameness rather than valuing individual expression. Certain themes in the book may be familiar to readers of Lowry's other novels.

Throughout *The Giver*, Lowry attempts to awaken each and every reader to the dangers that exist when people opt for conformity over individuality and for unexamined security over freedom. At one time in the past, the people who inhabited Jonas' community intended to create a perfect society. They thought that by protecting the citizens from making wrong choices (by having no choices), the community would be safe. But the utopian ideals went awry, and people became controlled and manipulated through social conditioning and language. Now, even the expression "love" is an empty ideal. For example, when Jonas asks his parents if they love him, his mother scolds him for using imprecise language. She says that "love" is "a very generalized word, so meaningless that it's become almost obsolete." To Jonas, however, love is a very real feeling.

Lowry stresses the point that people must not be blindly obedient to the rules of society. They must be aware of and must question everything about their lives. In Jonas' community, the people passively accept all rules and customs. They never question the fact that they are killing certain babies simply because such babies are different, or that they are killing old people whom they determine are no longer productive to the community. The community members unquestioningly follow rules; over time, because killing has become a routine practice, horrible and senseless actions do not morally, emotionally, or ethically upset them. As The Giver says of Jonas' father's killing the lighter-weight twin male, "It's what he was told to do, and he knows nothing else."

Theme

Another important theme in *The Giver* is the value of the individual. Lowry points out that when people are unable to experience pain, their individuality is devalued. Memories are so vital because they oftentimes include pain, and pain is an individual reaction: What is painful to one person might not be painful to another person. Also, people learn from memories and gain wisdom from remembering past experiences.

Character Insight

The people who live in Jonas' community are not individuals. Their lives are very routine, predictable, and unchanging. Because they chose Sameness generations ago, they gave up their individuality—and their freedom. Now, they know no other way of life.

Theme

Other themes in *The Giver*, such as family and home, friendships, acts of heroism, as well as the value of remembering the past, are familiar because they are themes in Lowry's previous novels also. Like Rabble in *Rabble Starkey*, Jonas has to leave the family that was created for him. Through the experience of leaving, both Jonas and Rabble learn to appreciate what it means to have a family and a home. And like Annemarie in Lowry's award winning *Number the Stars*, Jonas lives in a repressed society in which he has no freedom. Both Jonas and Annemarie risk their lives in order to save people they love. Because the conclusion of *The Giver* is so ambiguous, we don't know how Jonas' experiences ultimately affect him or his community.

Lowry challenges her readers to reexamine their values and to be aware of the interdependence of all human beings with each other, their environment, and the world in which they live. When people are forced to live under an oppressive regime that controls every person's actions, meaningful relationships between people are threatened because they involve individual feelings and thoughts. Only by questioning the conditions under which we live, as Jonas does in *The Giver*, can we maintain and secure our freedom of expression.

About the Characters

Jonas

Jonas is the protagonist, or main character, in the novel. He is a sensitive, polite, compassionate 12-year-old boy. Jonas is a dynamic character. He changes during the course of the novel due to his experiences and actions. We know how Jonas changes because Lowry narrates *The Giver* in the third person, limited omniscient viewpoint in order to reveal Jonas' thoughts and feelings. When the novel begins, Jonas is as unconcerned as anyone else about how he is living. He has grown up with loudspeakers, rules, precise language, and a family that is not connected biologically. He has accepted this way of life, because he doesn't know any other type of existence.

At the December Ceremony, Jonas is selected to become the new Receiver of Memory, the most honored position in the community. As he receives the Giver's memories and wisdom, he learns the truth about his community, that it is a hypocrisy and that the people have voluntarily given up their individuality and freedom to live as robots. Jonas' character changes and becomes more complex. He experiences an inner conflict because he misses his old life, his childhood, and his innocence, but he can't return to his former way of life because he has learned too much about joy, color, and love. Jonas knows that his life can never be "ordinary" again.

Jonas is also frustrated and angry because he wants his fellow citizens to change and thereby give up Sameness. He knows that the community and each person's life will benefit if only they would—or could—reclaim their individuality. Jonas realizes that his life would no longer be worth living if he were to continue living in the community as it is. To save the people in the community from their own senseless inhumanity, Jonas, an extremely courageous and brave character, risks his life. He flees the community with the baby, Gabriel. Jonas is afraid, but he is prepared to fight for their survival. Although we do not know how Jonas' experiences ultimately affect him or his community, we do know that he matures and that he feels excited and joyful as he and Gabriel ride down the hill on the sled.

The Giver

The Giver, an elderly man with a beard and pale eyes like Jonas', is the current Receiver of Memory. He carries the burden of the memories of the world, and suffers from the pain contained within the memories. Because The Giver is unable to share his work with anyone in the community (they would never understand), he is lonely. His life is totally different from the lives of other citizens in the community. He lives in rooms called the Annex, rooms unlike the dwellings of the other community members. He can lock his door and turn off the speaker; he has luxurious fabrics on his furniture and walls lined with shelves from top to bottom, holding thousands of books. These amenities isolate The Giver from other people living in the community.

The Giver is cynical and frustrated because he knows that the people gave up too much when they chose Sameness. As The Giver begins to transmit memories to Jonas, Jonas becomes upset. The Giver is surprised at the intensity of Jonas' feelings and the insight that Jonas already has about the philosophy of Sameness. Jonas mirrors the feelings The Giver has had for years. He admits that he's "never been able to think of a way" to force the people to accept memories, a statement that indicates that The Giver, like Jonas, wants to do away with Sameness in the community.

The Giver works with Jonas to develop a plan to do away with Sameness. He agrees to be available to help the people cope with their newly found memories. However, that is not enough for The Giver. He longs to be with his daughter, Rosemary, the earlier Receiver-in-Training who chose release over living a lonely and isolated life like The Giver. The Giver is telling Jonas that he intends to commit suicide. Because Lowry has written an ambiguous ending to the novel, we don't know what happens to The Giver.

Mother

Jonas' mother is an intelligent, sympathetic, and understanding person. She holds a prominent position at the Department of Justice. One of her job responsibilities is to punish people for breaking the strictly enforced rules of the community. According to Jonas, "her work never seem[s] to end." She always works after the family has had their evening meal.

Jonas' mother is proud that he has been named the new Receiver. She understands that it is the most prestigious position in the community, but, like other community members, she is unaware of the work Jonas will be doing. Throughout the novel, nothing seems to faze Jonas' mother. She systematically follows the rules of the community and, at the conclusion of the novel, she is exactly the same as she was at the beginning.

Father

Jonas' father is a shy, quiet, considerate, caring man. He is a Nurturer, responsible for the physical and emotional needs of every newborn child during the first few months of life. He is also responsible for the release (killing) of infants who are deemed worthless because something is emotionally and/or physically wrong with them.

Jonas' father does give the newborns every opportunity to flourish. He takes the newborn Gabriel home to live with his family in hopes of enabling the baby to sleep during the night and gain weight, thereby foregoing release.

Like other community members, Jonas' father follows the rules of the community. He is also a static, unchanging character.

Lily

Lily is Jonas' younger sister. She is a typically impatient child with straightforward, fairly simple feelings. Lily is also a chatterbox, talking continuously about subjects of interest to her. She is unconcerned about neatness, her hair ribbons are always untied, and because she is only seven (she becomes an Eight at the December Ceremony), she has many rules yet to learn.

Lily and Jonas behave like most brothers and sisters. They tease and become annoyed with one another from time to time. After Jonas has started to receive memories from the Giver, he tries to give Lily the memory of the *being* of an elephant (her comfort object is a stuffed elephant), but Lily complains that Jonas is hurting her because he is holding her shoulders too tightly. Lily is uninterested and unable to understand what Jonas implies when he talks to her about the fact that real elephants actually existed. She is also a one-dimensional character in *The Giver*.

Asher

Asher is Jonas' best friend. He is a cheerful, friendly boy who makes a game out of everything. Asher has always had trouble following the rules perfectly. He is often late for school and, as a result, has had to make numerous public apologies. The people in the community easily forgive Asher for his imperfections, because they like and enjoy him.

At the Ceremony of Twelve, Asher is assigned to be Assistant Director of Recreation. Because Jonas is selected to be the new Receiver of Memory, an honored position in the community, Asher is unsure how he should treat his friend and is hesitant to treat Jonas as he did during their years growing up together.

Fiona

Fiona is one of Jonas' good friends. She is a very pretty girl who is sensitive, intelligent, quiet, and polite. At the Ceremony of Twelve, Fiona is assigned to be Caretaker of the Old. Jonas accompanies Fiona as they ride their bicycles to their new assignments. Fiona talks to Jonas about her assignment and the new tasks that she will have to learn. Unfortunately, Jonas can not talk about his assignment as the Receiver of Memory. Jonas realizes that their relationship will change; however, Fiona is not emotionally affected by Jonas' silence. She is a static character—nothing happens *within* Fiona, things happen *to* her.

The Community Members

The people who live in Jonas' community are very predictable and unchanging. These characters are uncomplicated and complacent. They are static, simple, one-dimensional characters. Because the majority of them do not change throughout the novel, we see only one part of their personalities—their surface appearances and actions. Nothing happens *within* static characters; things happen *to* them.

Most of the citizens in the community passively follow the rules of the community. They always do what they are told by the Committee of Elders, following the rules and reprimands that are blasted over the loudspeakers located throughout the community and in every family dwelling. The people are totally controlled by the Committee of Elders as a result of a decision, a long time ago, to choose Sameness over individuality. The lives of the community members have been exactly the same for years. Nothing has ever happened to them except when an earlier Receiver-in-training, Rosemary, asked for release because she no longer could tolerate living in the community. After her death, the people were in total chaos because they didn't know what to do with the memories that Rosemary had experienced. They were not accustomed to thinking for themselves. Experiencing Rosemary's memories was something that happened to the people. Afterward, they resumed their lives as before, so it is evident that nothing permanently changed within them. Because Lowry has written an ambiguous ending, the changes that might have occurred as a result of Jonas' departure from the community are left to the imagination of each reader.

Activities for Readers

1. Write a newspaper article describing what happened to Jonas' community after he left with Gabe.

2. In the past, and especially in the nineteenth century, utopian communities such as Brook Farm, New Harmony, Oneida, and Shaker settlements were established in the United States. Research one of these communities and then compare it to Jonas' community.

3. Compare Jonas' community to Nazi Germany under Hitler.

4. Develop a plan for a utopian community. Include the name of your community, describe the government, the physical setting, and things that have been removed from or incorporated into your community.

Additional Resources

Campbell, Patty. "Sand in the Oyster." *The Horn Book Magazine.* November–December 1993: 717.

Chaston, Joel D. *Lois Lowry.* New York: Twayne Publishers, 1997.

Children's Literature Review. Vol. 46. Detroit: Gale Research, 1998: 25.

Contemporary Authors New Revision Series. Vol. 13. Detroit: Gale Research, 1984: 333–336.

Contemporary Authors New Revision Series. Vol. 43. Detroit: Gale Research, 1994: 280–282.

Dinuzzo, Toni, et.al. "Learning About Lois Lowry." *Young Adult Literature.* Internet. `www.scils.rutgers.edu/special/kay/lowry.html`.

Donelson, Kenneth, L., and Alleen Pace Nilsen. *Literature for Today's Young Adults*. New York: Addison-Wesley Educational Publishers, Inc., 1997.

"Euthanasia." *Microsoft Encarta 97 Encyclopedia*. CD-ROM. Microsoft Corporation, 1993–1996.

Flowers, Ann. "*The Giver*." *The Horn Book Magazine*. July–August 1993: 458.

"Infanticide." *Microsoft Encarta 97 Encyclopedia*. CD-ROM. Microsoft Corporation, 1993–1996.

"Lois Lowry." *Internet Public Library*. Online. www.ipl.org/youth/Ask Author/Biographies.html.

"Lois Lowry." *Mountain Brook City Schools*. Online. www.mtnbrook. k12.al.us/wf98/llowry2.htm.

Lorraine, Walter. "Lois Lowry." *The Horn Book Magazine*. July–August 1994: 423.

"Utopias." *Microsoft Encarta 97 Encyclopedia*. CD-ROM. Microsoft Corporation, 1993–1996.

MISSING MAY (1993)

Life and Background of the Author

Cynthia Rylant is an award-winning author of picture books, short stories, fiction, and poetry for children and young adults. Her style is clear, straightforward, and lyrical. Rylant's protagonists tend to be misfits—characters who are unusual due to their circumstances and, as a result, receive negative attention from others and are unappreciated. Rylant portrays these characters as unique, wonderful, valuable human beings. She focuses on interpersonal relationships between generations and on the hardships and joys of family life. Although Rylant writes about serious subjects, such as aging and death, and her characters lead challenging lives, she is able to interject humor, which lightens the tone and conveys hope and understanding to her readers. Rylant's childhood experiences, as well as the environment of rural West Virginia, influence her writing.

Rylant was born on June 6, 1954, in Hopewell, Virginia, to John Tune, an Army sergeant, and Leatrel Rylant Smith. Her parents, who had an unhappy marriage, divorced when she was four years old. Her mother took Rylant to live with her grandparents in Cool Ridge, West Virginia, while her mother attended nursing school. Rylant's grandparents' four-room house, which was on a dirt road away from the main highway, had no running water or electricity. The house was often shared with cousins, aunts, and uncles. Rylant's grandparents grew and hunted most of the food they ate. Because the family had no car, Rylant never traveled very far from home.

Rylant's father wrote letters to her occasionally when she first went to live with her grandparents, but after a while the letters stopped. Because none of her family members ever spoke about her father, Rylant did not have the courage to ask them about him. After several years, Rylant's father contacted her again. She looked forward to a reunion with her father, but before that could happen, he died. Rylant was 13 years old. The loss of her father, and not having had the opportunity to know him, affected Rylant deeply.

When Rylant was eight years old, she and her mother moved to Beaver, West Virginia. They lived in a small apartment near the railroad tracks. Rylant was happy in Beaver. She remembers having fun riding bikes and playing Tin Can Alley. Rylant doesn't remember being read to as a child, and didn't do much reading herself because there weren't many books available. There were no libraries, bookstores, or money to buy books. Rylant read *Archie and Jughead* comic books and Nancy Drew books. When she got older, she resorted to paperback romance novels. It wasn't until she went to college that she began to read literature.

In 1975, Rylant received a Bachelor of Arts degree from Morris Harvey College (now known as the University of Charleston) and, in 1976, she received a Master of Arts degree from Marshall University in West Virginia. Because Rylant thoroughly enjoyed books and reading, she thought she would become an English teacher, but after finishing college she couldn't find a teaching job. She worked as a waitress and then got a job at the Cabell County Public Library in Huntington, West Virginia, in the children's department. Until that time, Rylant had not been exposed to children's books. Her job as a librarian changed her life. Rylant loved reading children's books and within a short time she began to write children's stories. Her first book, *When I Was Young in the Mountains* (1982), was accepted for publication in 1978, just two months after she had submitted it to a publisher in New York. That same year, Rylant gave birth to her son, Nate (she had been married and divorced). Rylant and her son moved to Ohio, and, in 1982, she received a Master of Library Science degree from Kent State University. Rylant has taught English as a part-time lecturer at various universities.

Writing comes easily for Rylant. She writes picture books in one sitting. Her longer books take her about six months to write. She sometimes goes months without writing anything and then may "sense" a story in her mind, and simply sit down and write it. Many of Rylant's books are connected to her childhood and the West Virginia environment in which she grew up. Authors that have become role models for Rylant include Donald Hall, William Maxwell, Harper Lee, Fred Chappell, and James Agee in particular.

Rylant has received much acclaim for her writing. She won the Newbery Medal for *Missing May* (1992); two of her picture books, *When I Was Young in the Mountains* (1982) and *The Relatives Came* (1986), received the Caldecott Award; and *A Fine White Dust* (1986) was named a Newbery Honor Book. Three of Rylant's books—*A Kindness* (1988), *Soda Jerk* (1990), and *A Couple of Kooks and Other Stories about Love* (1990)—were named Best Book of the Year for Young Adults by the American Library Association.

Rylant, her son Nate, and all of their pets (dogs, cats, a parakeet, a guinea pig, and a hermit crab) moved to Eugene, Oregon, when Nate was 14 years old. They live in the same small green house in the woods today. Rylant enjoys reading, going to movies, watching public television, and, most of all, staying home spending time with her son, her friend Dav Pilkey, and all of their pets. Her life is quiet and simple, and that is the way she likes it. Although Rylant feels privileged to be a writer, she is unsure whether she will write books for the rest of her life. She is content, however, with the work she has accomplished and feels as though the words she has written have contributed to making the earth more beautiful for other people.

Rylant's Selected Works

When I Was Young in the Mountains (1982)

Miss Maggie (1983)

This Year's Garden (1984)

Waiting to Waltz: A Childhood (1984)

A Blue-Eyed Daisy (1985)

Every Living Thing (1985)

The Relatives Came (1985)

A Fine White Dust (1986)

Night in the Country (1986)

Children of Christmas: Stories for the Season (1987)

Birthday Presents (1987)

Henry and Mudge: The First Book of Their Adventures (1987)

Henry and Mudge in Puddle Trouble: The Second Book of Their Adventures (1987)

Henry and Mudge in the Green Time: The Third Book of Their Adventures (1987)

Henry and Mudge Under the Yellow Moon: The Fourth Book of Their Adventures (1987)

All I See (1988)

A Kindness (1988)

Henry and Mudge in the Sparkle Days: The Fifth Book of Their Adventures (1988)

But I'll Be Back Again: An Album (1989)

Henry and Mudge and the Forever Sea: The Sixth Book of Their Adventures (1989)

Henry and Mudge Get the Cold Shivers: The Seventh Book of Their Adventures (1989)

Mr. Griggs' Work (1989)

A Couple of Kooks and Other Stories about Love (1990)

Henry and Mudge and the Happy Cat: The Eighth Book of Their Adventures (1990)

Soda Jerk (1990)

Appalachia: The Voices of Sleeping Birds (1991)

Henry and Mudge and the Bedtime Thumps: The Ninth Book of Their Adventures (1991)

Henry and Mudge Take the Big Test: The Tenth Book of Their Adventures (1991)

An Angel for Solomon Singer (1992)

Best Wishes (1992)

Henry and Mudge and the Long Weekend: The Eleventh Book of Their Adventures (1992)

Missing May (1992)

The Dreamer (1993)

Henry and Mudge and the Wild Wind: The Twelfth Book of Their Adventures (1993)

I Had Seen Castles (1993)

Henry and Mudge and the Careful Cousin: The Thirteenth Book of Their Adventures (1994)

Mr. Putter and Tabby Bake the Cake (1994)

Mr. Putter and Tabby Pour the Tea (1994)

Mr. Putter and Tabby Walk the Dog (1994)

Something Permanent, with photographs by Walker Evans (1994)

Dog Heaven (1995)

Gooseberry Park (1995)

Henry and Mudge and the Best Day of All: The Fourteenth Book of Their Adventures (1995)

Mr. Putter and Tabby Pick the Pears (1995)

The Van Gogh Café (1995)

The Bookshop Dog (1996)

Margaret, Frank, and Andy: Three Writers' Stories (1996)

The Old Woman Who Named Things (1996)

The Whales (1996)

The Blue Hill Meadows (1997)

The Blue Hill Meadows and the Much-Loved Dog (1997)

Cat Heaven (1997)

An Everyday Book (1997)

Henry and Mudge in the Family Trees: The Fifteenth Book of Their Adventures (1997)

Mr. Putter and Tabby Fly the Plane (1997)

Mr. Putter and Tabby Row the Boat (1997)

Poppleton (1997)

Poppleton and Friends (1997)

Silver Packages: An Appalachian Christmas Story (1997)

Bear Day (1998)

The Bird House (1998)

Bless Us All: A Child's Yearbook of Blessings (1998)

The Cobble Street Cousins: In Aunt Lucy's Kitchen (1998)

The Cobble Street Cousins: A Little Shopping (1998)

Henry and Mudge and the Sneaky Crackers: The Sixteenth Book of Their Adventures (1998)

Henry and Mudge and the Starry Night: The Seventeenth Book of Their Adventures (1998)

Henry and Mudge and Annie's Good Move: The Eighteenth Book of Their Adventures (1998)

The Islander: A Novel (1998)

Mr. Putter and Tabby Take the Train (1998)

Mr. Putter and Tabby Toot the Horn (1998)

Poppleton Everyday (1998)

Poppleton Forever (1998)

Scarecrow (1998)

Tulip Sees America (1998)

Bunny Bungalow (1999)

The Cobble Street Cousins: Some Good News (1999)

The Cobble Street Cousins: Special Gifts (1999)

The Cookie-Store Cat (1999)

Give Me Grace: A Child's Daybook of Prayers (1999)

The Heavenly Village (1999)

Henry and Mudge and Annie's Perfect Pet: The Nineteenth Book of Their Adventures (1999)

Henry and Mudge and the Funny Lunch: The Twentieth Book of Their Adventures (1999)

Henry and Mudge and the Tall Tree House: The Twenty-First Book of Their Adventures (1999)

Henry and Mudge and Mrs. Hopper's House: The Twenty-Second Book of Their Adventures (1999)

Henry and Mudge and the Great Grandpas: The Twenty-Third Book of Their Adventures (1999)

Henry and Mudge and a Very Special Christmas: The Twenty-Fourth Book of Their Adventures (1999)

Henry and Mudge and the Snowman Plan: The Twenty-Fifth Book of Their Adventures (1999)

Henry and Mudge and the Wild Goose Chase: The Twenty-Sixth Book of Their Adventures (1999)

Henry and Mudge and the Big Sleepover: The Twenty-Seventh Book of Their Adventures (1999)

Henry and Mudge and the Tumbling Trip: The Twenty-Eighth Book of Their Adventures (1999)

Poppleton in Fall (1999)

Poppleton in Spring (1999)

The High Rise Private Eyes: The Case of the Climbing Cat (2000)

The High Rise Private Eyes: The Case of the Missing Monkey (2000)

In November (2000)

Let's Go Home: The Wonderful Things About a House (2000)

Little Whistle (2000)

Mr. Putter and Tabby Paint the Porch (2000)

Poppleton Through and Through (2000)

Thimbleberry Stories (2000)

The Wonderful Happens (2000)

A Brief Synopsis

Theme

Rylant wrote *Missing May* in the first person, revealing the thoughts and feelings of the grieving protagonist, Summer, who goes to live with her Aunt May and Uncle Ob when she is six years old. Summer's mother has died and none of her mother's brothers and sisters in Ohio want to be bothered with her. When she arrives at the run-down trailer in Deep River, West Virginia, that Ob and May call home, Summer discovers a family of her own—and enough love to last her a life time.

Literary Device

For six years, Summer feels like "she's died and gone to heaven." Her life is perfect. May takes care of Summer and Ob and enjoys her "gardening." Ob creates whirligigs that represent abstract ideas or things such as May's spirit, hope, heaven, love, dreams, and death, which they call *The Mysteries*. Summer goes to school and lives what she considers to be a normal life. But when Summer is 12 years old, her world is turned upside down. May dies suddenly while working in her garden. Ob and Summer are devastated. They don't know how to go on without May. Within a short time, Ob reveals to Summer that May's spirit has visited him. Summer becomes concerned about Ob. She is afraid that Ob will want to be with May and that he will die and she will be left alone.

Cletus Underwood, a classmate of Summer's (who she would rather *not* be associated with), befriends Ob (and later, Summer). Cletus begins to spend a lot of time at their trailer listening to Ob tell about May's "visits." Cletus is nonjudgmental and is empathetic toward Ob. Because Cletus had a near-death experience as a small child, Ob becomes convinced that Cletus can help him communicate with May's spirit. Ob wants to install him like some "afterlife antenna." Cletus shows Ob an advertisement about a medium, named Reverend Young, who communicates with the dead. He suggests that they go to Putnam County to find Reverend Young and stop at the state capitol in Charleston on the way home. Ob, Cletus, and Summer look forward to the trip. Summer hopes that contacting May through Reverend Young will alleviate Ob's depression and give him a reason to keep going. They are crushed when they arrive in Putnam County only to discover that Reverend Young has died. Ob decides to return home. Summer and Cletus do not mention their plan to stop at the state capitol.

As they pass the capitol, "Right out of the blue, [Ob] wanted to live again." Not wanting to disappoint Summer and Cletus, he turns the car around and goes back to the capitol where they spend an enjoyable day. They return home that night and as they are taking their belongings out of the car (Cletus is going to spend the night), an owl flies overhead. The owl reminds summer of May and how much she misses her. Summer cries for the first time since May's death. The next morning, Ob, Summer, and Cletus take all of Ob's whirligigs out to May's garden where they erect them. They set the whirligigs free, along with May's spirit, and find consolation in their memories of May.

Character Map

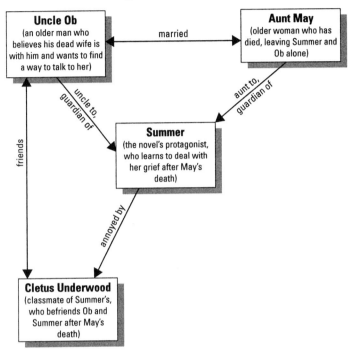

Geography

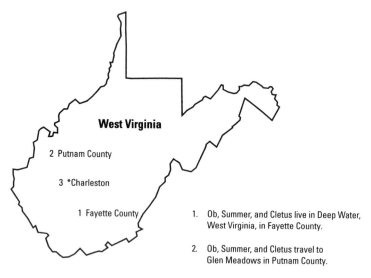

West Virginia

2 Putnam County

3 *Charleston

1 Fayette County

1. Ob, Summer, and Cletus live in Deep Water, West Virginia, in Fayette County.

2. Ob, Summer, and Cletus travel to Glen Meadows in Putnam County.

3. Ob, Summer, and Cletus stop in Charleston to visit the state capitol.

Major Themes

Theme

The controlling theme of *Missing May* is grief and the grieving process. Grief is the natural reaction to loss; it is a universal experience encountered many times throughout a person's life. May's death was a physical, or tangible, loss for Ob and Summer. According to Summer, "all Ob and me wanted to do when we lost May was hold onto each other and wail in that trailer for days and days." They weren't able to do that because "there are certain ways people expect you to grieve." Summer and Ob had a funeral ritual for May and acted "proper" in front of relatives and people they didn't even know. After the funeral, Ob and Summer began the grieving process in their own way and time.

Character Insight

One way to understand the grieving process is to view it as tasks or stages that people move through after they have experienced a loss. At first, they must accept the reality of the loss. To deal with the loss, people might choose isolation or denial. Both Summer and Ob chose denial. Summer denied her feelings related to May's death and absence.

She attempted to fill May's shoes. The responsibility of taking care of Ob kept her occupied, so she didn't have to deal with her feelings about the loss of May. After May died, Ob denied that she was really gone. He felt her presence and believed she was with them.

The next task or stage has to do with experiencing the pain or grief. Summer did not experience the pain of May's death until the night they returned home from their journey to Putnam County. She saw an owl and was reminded of May. Summer cried until "[her] body was emptied of those tears and [she] was [no longer] burdened." Ob experienced the pain of May's death by becoming depressed. He didn't feel he had a reason to live without May. He struggled to get out of bed each day and one day he didn't even get dressed; he stayed in his pajamas. After Summer and Ob experienced their grief, they were able to accept May's death and look forward to adjusting to life without May.

In the characters of Ob and Summer, Rylant portrays the anguish and despair that people experience as a result of loss due to death. Rylant makes it clear that grieving is unique to each individual, the length of time each person grieves varies greatly, and hope and understanding enable people to be able to move on with their lives.

Another important theme in *Missing May* is the importance of family. Rylant suggests that a family does not have to include a biological mother, father, and children to be a family. She portrays unconventional families—families that are not traditional. One family that is unconventional is Summer's family. She lives with her elderly Aunt May (until she dies) and Uncle Ob. This is a perfect family for Summer: She feels safe, secure, and loved. Cletus' family is also unconventional. Although his parents are elderly people, Cletus also feels safe, secure, and loved. Rylant portrays the "darker" side of family life when she writes about a dysfunctional family—a family that includes conflict and poor relationships among family members. An example of a dysfunctional family is Summer's extended family in Ohio. After her mother died, her aunts and uncles didn't want her. They "treated [her] like a homework assignment somebody was always having to do."

Valuing the differences in others is another significant theme of *Missing May*. When Cletus began to visit Ob, Summer considered him to be a lunatic. It wasn't until she observed the way that he listened to and empathized with Ob that her opinion of Cletus changed. She realized he had "gifts." Summer was also a victim of people making incorrect assumptions about her. Her teacher asked the class to write descriptions of each other. Someone wrote a description about Summer that made her sound "like some sad welfare case, in the sorry way her clothes and hair were described." Summer's reaction was an urge to run home to Ob and May where she knew she would be safe. May was a good role model for Summer. May naturally thought the best of everyone and everything. She never judged anyone or anything. She "always liked the weird ones best." Summer was sure May would have liked Cletus. May even saw the beauty in bats; she treated them gently and lovingly.

Rylant hopes that by exposing her readers to grief as a natural reaction to loss resulting from death, the importance of family, and the uniqueness and value of every individual, she can bring awareness to her readers and thereby change perceptions and, ultimately, the society in which we live.

About the Characters

The characters in *Missing May* are static characters. They don't change much throughout the novel. Even though something happens to them (May dies), their characters are the same at the end of the novel as they are at the beginning.

Summer

Summer is the protagonist, or main character, of the novel. Because Rylant has written *Missing May* in the first person, Summer tells the story from her perspective as she experiences and understands it. Summer spent the first six years of her life in Ohio. After her mother died, she was passed around among her aunts and uncles. Summer knew that nobody wanted her, but that didn't dampen her spirit. She saved the love that she imagined was in her heart, given to her by her mother, for people who wanted to love her. When she met her Aunt May and Uncle Ob, things clicked, and it was love at first sight. She went home, to West Virginia, with her Aunt May and Uncle Ob to live with them in their broken down trailer. Summer was elated. May and Ob doted on her, treating her as though she was their very own child. She loved them and their eccentric ways as much as they loved her. She felt as though she had "died and gone to heaven."

Summer is 12 years old when Aunt May dies. She misses May terribly and is aware that Ob does, too. Summer recognizes that she and Ob are "not strong" anymore. She assumes the responsibility for trying to mend Ob's broken heart (an impossible task) in an attempt to hold onto as much of the old, familiar, comfortable life that she had known with May and Ob.

Cletus Underwood befriends Ob, and eventually, Summer. At first, Summer resents Cletus' presence. She is jealous of Cletus because he puts a sparkle in Ob's eyes when she can't. Over time, she begins to appreciate Cletus and is grateful for his attention to Ob. Because Ob spends more and more time talking to Cletus, Summer feels as though she has been left to fend for herself and she doesn't know what to do about it.

Things seem to be spiraling out of Summer's control. Ob talks about seeing May and neglects to get up one morning. Summer is afraid that if Ob falls apart, she will lose him and will then lose everything that she loves. She doesn't "know how to keep him tied to her." She feels as though they are both in a fog. She thinks the idea of going to Putnam County to see Reverend Young, a medium who talks to the dead, is crazy but she will do anything if it gives Ob the will to keep living.

Before going to Putnam County, Summer and Ob go to Cletus' house to get his parents permission to go with them. Summer realizes that Cletus has been ashamed of her because she has been reluctant to have anything to do with him (she thinks he is a little bit strange). She is embarrassed by her action. Since he has been spending time at their trailer, she has grown to respect Cletus and can now see the good in him.

The trip to Putnam County is peaceful for Summer. She is free of the responsibility of caring for everyone and everything—a burden that she placed on herself at the time of May's death. When they can't see Reverend Young (who has died) and talk to May, Ob is disappointed, and Summer is devastated. She thinks that Ob will give up on life because he can not see Reverend Young. She ". . . swallow[s] back the lump in [her] throat and pray[s] for something to save Ob and [her]."

When they get home, an owl flies over Summer's head and she remembers May. Over the past two seasons, she has been so concerned about Ob that she hasn't thought about May and hasn't been able to grieve for May. Finally, Summer realizes that May is gone and that she will never see May again. She cries her heart out for May. She accepts

May's death and is able to let go of her fears. For the first time in two seasons, she feels free and certain that neither she nor Ob is going to give up on the life they have together.

Uncle Ob

Ob is Summer's uncle, who was married to May. He looks like a scarecrow—tall and thin. Because May always made him feel special, Ob never felt bad about being a "disabled Navy man" (he has arthritis). Ob is an artist. He makes unusual whirligigs—he and May call them *The Mysteries.* They are his interpretation of abstract ideas or things, such as heaven, love, dreams, fire, or death. Summer describes Ob as "a deep thinker . . . [who] was often getting revelations." May's acceptance and appreciation of Ob's eccentricities gave him the confidence to be himself and to be a "free thinker."

Ob deals with May's death by sitting in his old Chevy all night. He is devastated. He loved May as much as a person can love another, and he doesn't know how to live without her. One day shortly after her death, Ob has a revelation that May is with them, that her spirit is visiting Summer and Ob. He becomes frustrated and sad when he doesn't feel her presence again.

Cletus Underwood, a classmate of Summer's who is quite unique (Summer thinks he is a lunatic), begins to visit Ob and Summer frequently. Ob likes Cletus and seems to be fascinated by him. Cletus' visits and stories distract Ob from his grief and Cletus listens to Ob without judging him or making comments. Unknowingly, Cletus is allowing Ob to grieve for May in his own way.

Ob becomes quite depressed (a normal part of the grieving process). He doesn't get out of bed one morning, and when he does get up, he stays in his pajamas all day, crying in front of Summer—all behaviors that are unusual for Ob.

When Cletus arrives at the trailer with a newspaper clipping about a minister in Putnam County who communicates with the dead, Ob thinks they should go find this minister so he can talk to May. He feels hopeful and finally has a reason to live. Because Cletus is included in the plan to go to Putnam County, Ob and Summer go to visit Cletus' parents to get permission for Cletus to accompany them. Ob doesn't tell the Underwoods the truth about why they are going to Putnam County—instead of telling them about Reverend Young, he says the reason they are going is to cheer up Summer. Ob understands people and knows that "not everybody is as free minded" as he and Summer.

On their journey to find Reverend Young, Ob is quiet. He is sad and fearful about what Reverend Young might tell him. When they find out the minister has died and they can't speak to May, they get back in the car. Ob is disappointed and wants to get back home. They get in the car and drive towards Fayette County—past the capitol. And then, "Right out of the blue, he want[s] to live again." Ob turns the car around and goes back to the capitol. Ob can't bear the thought of disappointing Summer and Cletus.

Ob has finally accepted May's death. Ob, Summer, and Cletus, in a ritual to say goodbye to May, put all of Ob's whirligigs in May's garden. May's spirit is finally free, and Ob is free to go on with his life.

Aunt May

May was Summer's aunt and Ob's husband. Rylant describes her as a "big woman" (she had to "hoist" herself out of the car) who loved to garden. When she died, she was in her garden.

May was a homebody. She enjoyed being home and feared that if she left their trailer, it wouldn't be there when she returned. She suffered significant losses during her lifetime. Her family was victim of a flood when she was nine years old. Everything was washed away, and her mother and father died. May had a strong belief in "spirits from the next world" and always felt as though her parents watched over her—until she met Ob. Then they could relax and fly "off to that big church picnic in the sky."

May was reliable and dependable. She took care of Ob and Summer and was happy doing it. She provided a positive environment in which Summer flourished. May was an optimistic person, always looking for the best in people, and, in return, people showed her their best side. May allowed people the freedom to live life to the fullest and to be who they were meant to be. She was good for Ob and Summer because she always focused on their strengths, which increased their self-esteem and made them feel as though they could do whatever they set their mind to. May would have been happy to know that Ob's special whirligigs were in her garden and that Ob and Summer were now holding onto each other.

Cletus Underwood

Cletus is one of Summer's classmates. He has long, straight, black hair that looks greasy (Summer doesn't think he bathes regularly), he has acne on his face, and he wears a funny looking hat that has ear flaps. Cletus is different from other people his age; Summer thinks he is a lunatic. He is a collector of unlikely items such as potato chip bags, buttons, spoons, plants, wrapping paper, and now, pictures that he carries with him in an old suitcase. Cletus uses his imagination to create stories for every picture.

Cletus first meets Ob and becomes acquainted with Summer when Ob notices him snooping around their old Chevy. As Summer and Ob grieve, Cletus becomes a "guide" for them in their search for May. Cletus and Ob become fast friends in spite of Summer's objections. Cletus seems to understand how devastating it has been for Ob to lose May. He begins visiting Ob and Summer often. Cletus' presence seems to have a positive impact on Ob, and Summer observes that Cletus has "some gifts." Cletus seems to live full of hope and confidence. He listens to Ob talk and is not judgmental. For example, when Ob stays in his pajamas all day, Cletus never comments; he simply ignores the fact that Ob has not gotten dressed all day. Cletus is insightful and perceptive. He tells Summer to "drop some of them bricks you keep hauling with you. Life just ain't that heavy." Cletus understands that Summer has taken on the responsibility of trying to fill May's shoes—a task that is impossible for her to accomplish. Cletus believes Summer is fighting herself and is not allowing herself to think freely or to be the writer he believes she is.

Cletus becomes Ob's "afterlife antenna." Because he had a near-death experience as a small child, Ob believes that Cletus' energy will attract May's spirit to visit again. Cletus shows Ob an advertisement for a medium—a spiritualist who speaks to the dead—named Reverend Young. Ob, Summer, and Cletus decide to take a trip to find her and possibly speak to May through her. Cletus is excited about the prospect of seeing the state capitol. He hasn't traveled much and, because he wants to be a "Renaissance Man," he sees the trip as an opportunity to move towards his goal.

After finding out that Reverend Young is no longer alive and after visiting the capitol, with which he is enthralled, Cletus goes home with Ob and Summer. He spends the night with them at their trailer, and then accompanies Ob and Summer to May's garden to help erect Ob's whirligigs. Cletus blesses the whirligigs by reading from Reverend Young's brochure. Unknowingly, Cletus has been a consoling presence for Ob and Summer during their grieving process.

Activities for Readers

1. Research the stages of grief. List ways in which you can help others cope with grief.

2. Rylant uses symbols throughout Missing May such as Ob's whirligigs, an owl, May's garden, and a crow flying overhead. What do these items symbolize or represent? Find other examples of symbols in the book and decide what abstract ideas they represent.

3. After Summer's mother died, Summer lived with various aunts and uncles until she was taken in by Ob and May. Summer called Ob and May her family. What is a family? What are the characteristics of a family?

4. Rylant uses rural West Virginia as a setting for many of her books because she grew up there and that environment made an indelible impression on her. Think about the environment in which you spent your childhood. Describe the environment in which you grew up as a setting for a possible story.

5. Ob made whirligigs that were representations of abstract ideas or things, such as heaven, fire, hope, death, and May's spirit. Create a whirligig of your own that is a representation of an abstract noun.

6. Compare and contrast Summer's grieving process to Ob's grieving process. How was the process the same? How was the process different?

Additional Resources

Children's Literature Review. Vol. 15. Detroit: Gale Research, 1988: 167–174.

"Middle School Book Club Unit Plan for Missing May by Cynthia Rylant. Small Planet Communications. Online. www.smplanet.com/ bookclub/MissingMay/mayintro.html.

Ramsey, Inez and Wilburn, Herb. Cynthia Rylant. Online. falcon. jmu.edu/~ramseyil/rylant.htm.

Ruthven, Beverly and Rogers, Sue F. "Missing May." *Beacham's Desktop Guide to Literature for Intermediate Students.* Florida: Beacham Publishing, 1995: 256–261.

Rylant, Cynthia. *But I'll Be Back Again: An Album.* New York: Orchard Books, 1989.

Rylant, Cynthia. "Missing May." *The Horn Book Magazine.* January–February 1993: 52–53.

Rylant, Cynthia. "Newbery Medal Acceptance." *The Horn Book Magazine.* July–August 1993: 416–419.

"Rylant, Cynthia." Educational Paperback Association. Online. www.edupaperback.org/authorbios/rylantc.html.

Ward, Diane. "Cynthia Rylant." *The Horn Book Magazine.* July–August 1993: 420–423.

SHILOH (1992)

Life and Background of the Author

Phyllis Reynolds Naylor is an American author and journalist. She has been described as prolific (she has written over one hundred books, most of which are for children and young adults) and versatile (she writes picture books, fiction, nonfiction, and instruction books). Her protagonists, or main characters, are strong, honest, determined characters that mature as a result of having prevailed despite adversity. Naylor's books portray her understanding of the trials and tribulations of childhood and adolescence. She writes about serious issues such as mental illness in *The Keeper*, crib death in *A Story of Chances*, and difficult moral questions in *Shiloh*. She also writes humorous mysteries (the *Bessledorf* series) and books about the supernatural (the York trilogy and the Witch trilogy). Naylor hopes that by writing about sensitive topics and exposing her readers to characters and ideas that are different, she can encourage them to become more open minded.

Naylor was born on January 4, 1933, in Anderson, Indiana, to Eugene S. Reynolds and Lura Schield Reynolds. Her family moved many times during her childhood because her father was a traveling salesman; consequently, Naylor doesn't consider any single place "home." She spent summer vacations with her grandparents. Her paternal grandparents (her father's parents), openly warm and affectionate people, lived in Maryland and her maternal grandparents (her mother's parents), no-nonsense people who reserved hugs for arrivals and departures, lived in Iowa. Naylor's summer visits made an impression on her; she has relied on memories of Maryland and Iowa to create settings and characters for several of her books.

Even though Naylor grew up during the Depression and her family was not well off, she never felt poor. Her family owned a number of good books and she recalls her parents reading aloud to her and her siblings daily until they were adolescents. They read the Bible storybook, Grimm's fairy tales, *Alice in Wonderland*, all of Mark Twain's books, *The Wind in the Willows*, and others. During elementary school, Naylor's favorite hobby was to "write" her own books, and by the time she was 16 years old, her first story was published in a church magazine.

Naylor married in 1951 at the age of 18. Two years later, in 1953, she graduated from Joliet Junior College and moved to Chicago with her husband. She worked as a secretary while her husband attended graduate school. During the next few years it became evident that her husband had a severe mental illness that was later diagnosed as paranoid schizophrenia. Because her husband was unable to work, Naylor supported them with income from her writing. She also worked briefly as an elementary school teacher, as an assistant executive secretary, and as an editorial assistant with the *NEA Journal*, a publication of the National Education Association. Naylor eventually obtained a divorce from her first husband and, in 1960, married Rex V. Naylor, a speech pathologist.

Naylor returned to college to major in clinical psychology. She attended American University and received her Bachelor of Arts degree in 1963. While in school, Naylor wrote stories to pay her tuition. After graduating, she decided to focus on becoming a full-time writer rather than pursue a graduate degree. Within two years, Naylor's first book, *The Galloping Goat and Other Stories* (1965), nine short stories about children in other lands, was published. Since then, she has written over one hundred books and won numerous awards. Many of her books have been given special recognition by the American Library Association and the International Reading Association, and have been Junior Literary Guild selections. She has won two prestigious awards, the Edgar Allan Poe Award, received from the Mystery Writers of America in 1985 for *Night Cry* (1984), and the John Newbery Medal for *Shiloh* (1991).

Naylor does not have a problem coming up with ideas for her books; instead, other story ideas sometimes interfere with her writing. Her inspiration for writing is everything that she has ever experienced in her life, incidents that other people have experienced, and her imagination. She is usually writing more than one book at a time, and continually collects information for up to ten future book ideas. Naylor mixes up her writing to keep her job interesting and fun. For example, if she writes a humorous book, she might write a serious book next; if she writes a book for adults, she might write a picture book for children after that.

Today, Naylor lives in Bethesda, Maryland with her husband, Rex. They have two grown sons, Jeffrey Alan and Michael Scott. When she isn't writing, she enjoys going to the theater, reading, singing, playing the piano, hiking, swimming, and snorkeling. She reads books about ordinary people and books by southern authors. Although Naylor is extremely busy and productive in her personal life and with her writing, she manages to find time to be an active member in peace and civil rights organizations.

Naylor's Selected Works

The Galloping Goat (1965)

Grasshoppers in the Soup (1965)

Jennifer Jean, the Cross-Eyed Queen (1967)

Knee-Deep Ice Cream, and Other Stories (1967)

The New Schoolmaster (1967)

A New Year's Surprise (1967)

To Make a Shadow (1967)

What the Gulls Were Singing (1967)

When Rivers Meet (1968)

Dark Side of the Moon (1969)

Meet Murdock (1969)

The Private I, and Other Stories (1969)

To Make a Wee Moon (1969)

Making It Happen (1970)

Ships in the Night (1970)

How to Find Your Wonderful Someone; How to Keep Him/Her If You Do; How to Survive If You Don't (1971)

Wrestle the Mountain (1971)

No Easy Circle (1972)

To Walk the Sky Path (1973)

An Amish Family (1974)

Witch's Sister (1975)

Getting Along in Your Family (1976)

Walking through the Dark (1976)

Crazy Love: An Autobiographical Account of Marriage and Madness (1977)

Witch Water (1977)

How I Came to Be a Writer (1978)

The Witch Herself (1978)

How Lazy Can You Get? (1979)

In Small Doses (1979)

Revelations: A Novel (1979)

Change in the Wind (1980)

Eddie, Incorporated (1980)

Getting Along with Your Friends (1980)

Shadows on the Wall (1980)

All Because I'm Older (1981)

Faces in the Water (1981)

Footprints at the Window (1981)

Getting Along with Your Teachers (1981)

The Boy with the Helium Head (1982)

Never Born a Hero (1982)

A String of Chances (1982)

The Mad Gasser of Bessledorf Street (1983)

The Solomon System (1983)

Night Cry (1984)

Old Sadie and the Christmas Bear (1984)

A Triangle Has Four Sides (1984)

The Agony of Alice (1985)

The Dark of the Tunnel (1985)

The Bodies in the Bessledorf Hotel (1986)

The Keeper (1986)

Unexpected Pleasures (1986)

The Baby, the Bed, and the Rose (1987)

Beetles, Lightly Toasted (1987)

The Year of the Gopher (1987)

Maudie in the Middle, with Lura Schield Reynolds (1988)

One of the Third-Grade Thonkers (1988)

Alice in Rapture, Sort Of (1989)

The Craft of Writing the Novel (1989)

Keeping a Christmas Secret (1989)

A Traitor among the Boys (1989)

Bernie and the Bessledorf Ghost (1990)

Send No Blessings (1990)

The Witch's Eye (1990)

King of the Playground (1991)

Reluctantly Alice (1991)

Shiloh (1991)

Witch Weed (1991)

All but Alice (1992)

Josie's Troubles (1992)

The Witch Returns (1992)

Alice in April (1993)

The Boys Start the War (1993)

The Face in the Bessledorf Funeral Parlor (1993)

The Girls Get Even (1993)

The Grand Escape (1993)

Alice In-Between (1994)

Boys against Girls (1994)

The Fear Place (1994)

Alice the Brave (1995)

Being Danny's Dog (1995)

Ice (1995)

Alice in Lace (1996)

The Bomb in the Bessledorf Bus Depot (1996)

Shiloh Season (1996)

Ducks Disappearing (1997)

The Healing of Texas Jake (1997)

"I Can't Take You Anywhere!" (1997)

Outrageously Alice (1997)

Saving Shiloh (1997)

The Treasure of Bessledorf Hill (1997)

Achingly Alice (1998)

Danny's Desert Rats (1998)

The Girls' Revenge (1998)

Sang Spell (1998)

Alice on the Outside (1999)

Peril in the Bessledorf Parachute Factory (1999)

Sweet Strawberries (1999)

Walker's Crossing (1999)

Carlotta's Kittens and the Club of Mysteries (2000)

The Grooming of Alice (2000)

Jade Green: A Ghost Story (2000)

A Spy among the Girls (2000)

A Brief Synopsis

Shiloh is written in the first person point of view, revealing the thoughts and feelings of the determined and compassionate protagonist, Marty Preston. The novel begins when a young beagle follows 11-year-old Marty as he takes a walk up in the hills on the road past the old Shiloh schoolhouse near Friendly, West Virginia. Because the dog is "slinking down, . . . tail between his legs like he's hardly got the right to breathe" and backing off and cringing when Marty puts out his hand, he is sure the dog's owner is abusing him. Marty feels protective of the dog, and names him Shiloh.

Marty's father thinks the dog belongs to Judd Travers, who recently got another hunting dog. Marty doesn't like Judd or trust him. Marty saw Judd cheat Mr. Wallace in the corner store, Marty knows that Judd kills deer out of season, and he hates that Judd chews tobacco and tries to spit it close to people he doesn't like. When Marty's father takes him to Judd's trailer to return Shiloh, Marty sees Judd kick Shiloh and pleads with Judd to stop kicking the dog.

Marty can't stop thinking about Shiloh. He decides that he has to buy Shiloh from Judd. Unfortunately, there aren't very many jobs in Friendly for a boy his age. Marty starts collecting cans and bottles to try to make some money, but realizes it will take him forever to raise enough money to buy Shiloh. He also thinks about what he will feed Shiloh. Because his family is sending money to help care for his Grandma Preston, the family doesn't have any extra money to spend on dog food.

Before long, Shiloh runs away from Judd again and ends up at Marty's house. This time, Marty hides Shiloh in a makeshift pen just off the path that leads up the hill behind his house. He makes sure Shiloh has water and protection from the weather. Marty becomes attached to Shiloh as he continues to care for him—taking Shiloh on long walks, playing with him, and feeding him whatever he can manage to save from his own meals. Marty even swallows his pride and asks Mr. Wallace at the corner store for old food that he can buy cheap, just so Shiloh won't go hungry.

Marty's Ma discovers Marty's secret when she finds Marty with Shiloh in the pen one evening. She agrees to keep his secret until the next day, giving him time to decide what to do about Shiloh. That night, a German shepherd jumps into Shiloh's pen and attacks him. Marty's Dad takes Shiloh to Doc Murphy. Even though Doc Murphy is not a vet, he agrees to help Shiloh. Marty's Dad agrees to let him keep Shiloh until Shiloh is well, and then Shiloh will have to go back to Judd. Marty feels guilty. He feels it was his fault Shiloh was hurt because he didn't make the pen tall enough. He also feels relieved because his secret is out in the open and he has time to figure out how he can keep Shiloh.

The next day, Doc Murphy shows up with Shiloh. Marty's Ma tells Marty to get a box and put it in the kitchen for Shiloh. As Shiloh's condition improves, and he is able to hobble about, Marty's family slowly but surely falls in love with him. Marty is more determined than ever to keep Shiloh. He feels that his only option is to talk directly to Judd.

Early in the morning on the day Shiloh is to be returned to Judd, Marty cuts through the woods on his way to Judd's trailer. On his way, he catches Judd shooting a deer out of season. Marty knows that if the Warden finds out, Judd will be fined for shooting the deer. Marty confronts Judd, and, thinking quickly, he makes a bargain with Judd. He agrees to be silent about Judd shooting the doe in exchange for Shiloh. Marty also agrees to work for Judd twenty hours for two dollars an hour, in order to pay for Shiloh.

Character Insight

The work Marty does for Judd is difficult, backbreaking work; however, he attempts to do his best. During the time he works for Judd, Marty gains understanding about Judd and feels almost sorry for him. Marty can finally see Judd as a person who doesn't know how to care about other people or animals. Marty feels proud of himself for keeping up his end of their bargain in spite of the obstacles that Judd has put in his way. On the last day that Marty works for Judd, Judd gives Marty a collar for Shiloh and tells him, "you got yourself a dog." Marty's family celebrates the fact that Shiloh belongs to them and Marty realizes that "nothing is as simple as you guess."

Character Map

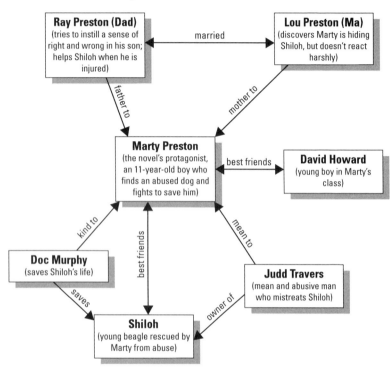

Major Themes

Major themes in *Shiloh* include justice, and determining what is right or wrong, and the importance of family and friends. Naylor used her personal experience—finding a silent, skinny, scared dog while taking a walk in West Virginia—to convey the notion that a person's perspective changes when he or she becomes emotionally involved in a problem.

The first time Marty whistles and Shiloh runs to him, wagging his tail, licking Marty's fingers and face, Marty's perspective about what is best for Shiloh becomes subjective. Marty becomes emotionally involved with Shiloh; he "got hooked on him." Marty's perspective causes him to feel responsible for Shiloh's welfare, even though Shiloh belongs to Judd Travers. Marty faces a moral dilemma that involves justice. He has to make a decision about what is right and what is wrong, and then act on his decision. In Marty's situation, the decision is not clear-cut. He hides Shiloh and keeps Shiloh's presence a secret from everyone. He struggles with knowing that he is doing what he thinks is best for Shiloh, but he is being dishonest with his family and with his good friend, David Howard. Marty feels guilty about the lies that he tells to protect Shiloh; however he justifies his lies because he truly believes that caring for Shiloh is what Jesus would want him to do. He prays to Jesus asking, "Which you want me to do? Be one hundred percent honest and carry that dog back to Judd so that one of your creatures can be kicked and starved all over again, or keep him here and fatten him up to glorify your creation?" To Marty, "a lie don't seem like a lie anymore when it's meant to save a dog." Life becomes complicated for Marty. He is being pulled in several different directions. He doesn't know what the boundary is between living strictly according to the law (which would mean giving Shiloh back to Judd because Judd legally owns Shiloh) or living according to what he feels is the right thing to do (protect Shiloh from Judd's abuse). Marty loves his family and has never lied to them before, but now, he also loves Shiloh.

Marty must figure out what to do based on his own sense of right and wrong, taking into consideration his family's values. Marty questions his parents by asking, "What kind of law is it . . . that lets a man mistreat his dog?" and "What's right?" Naylor points out that there are exceptions to every rule and that it is necessary throughout life to stand up for what you believe is fair and just and then be ready to compromise. Marty does compromise—using time to figure out how he can keep Shiloh. He agrees to take Shiloh back to Judd *after* Shiloh is well. Later, Marty also compromises with Judd. Marty agrees to work for Judd and keeps quiet about the fact that Judd shot a deer illegally in exchange for Shiloh. Throughout the process, Marty realizes that "nothing is as simple as you guess—not right or wrong. . . ."

Another major theme in *Shiloh* is the importance of family and friends. Family is a priority for the Prestons. Even though they don't have much money, they manage to send money to help Aunt Hettie care for Grandma Preston. When Marty goes on the postal route with his father, his father shows that he cares about Marty and has been paying attention to him by asking Judd questions about his dogs. Marty's father knows Marty is worried about Shiloh and he seems to know what to ask Judd to satisfy Marty's interest. When Marty's family discovers his secret (Shiloh) and realizes he has been lying to them, they are not happy about the lies, but they support him and assist him in righting a wrong. His parents stand beside him as he tells Doc Murphy and Judd the truth.

Marty's relationship with his friend, David, is also significant. Marty chose not to share his secret about Shiloh with David. When David did find out, he supported Marty and helped him clean out Shiloh's pen. Marty felt good having David's help because David's presence made the job easier and helped keep Marty from focusing on thoughts related to his guilt about the German shepherd attacking Shiloh. Marty thinks that he and David will be "friends for life." Being able to trust and depend on family and friends enables people to feel secure, thereby allowing each person in the relationship to flourish.

Naylor writes about the difficulties involved in deciding what is right and what is wrong and the value of family and friends to portray the notion that people are unique and naturally figure out solutions to life's dilemmas in their own way.

About the Characters

Marty

Marty is the protagonist, or main character, of the novel. He is an 11-year-old boy who lives with his parents and two younger sisters in a "four-room house with hills on three sides." Marty loves the woods and the meadows and the animals that inhabit the area. He takes his rifle out to shoot but "never shoot(s) at anything moving . . . never had the slightest wish." He can't eat rabbit that his father's killed because he can't stand the thought of the rabbit suffering, he encourages his sisters to release fireflies they capture and put in a jar, and he does all he can to protect a skinny, scared beagle that follows him home.

Marty is a dynamic character. He changes during the course of the novel due to his experiences and actions. Naylor narrates *Shiloh* in the first person, so we know how Marty changes because his thoughts and feelings are revealed. When the novel begins, the little beagle, that Marty names Shiloh, follows him home. Almost immediately, Marty falls in love with the dog. He is sure Shiloh came to him for help, and he intends to protect Shiloh from the abusive hands of Shiloh's owner, Judd Travers. When Marty goes with his Dad to take Shiloh back to Judd, Marty feels as though he has let Shiloh down, as though he has not protected Shiloh. He thinks about Shiloh night and day, trying to figure out how he can purchase the dog from Judd.

Within days, Shiloh shows up at Marty's house and Marty, determined to keep him, quickly builds a pen on the hill and keeps Shiloh's presence secret. As time passes, Marty experiences an inner conflict. He loves Shiloh and wants to protect the dog; however, he also loves his family and feels guilty about lying to them about where he goes and what he is doing with the leftover food from his dinner plate that he's giving to Shiloh. Marty learns from experience "that you can lie not only by what you say but what you don't say."

Marty lies to Judd about whether or not he has seen Shiloh in the yard (Shiloh has not been in the yard, he has been in the pen up the hill). Marty experiences a conflict with Judd because he wants Judd's dog and Judd wants his dog back. Marty also experiences a conflict with society—he doesn't understand laws that don't protect animals from mistreatment. Marty knows that he can't do anything about the laws in time to save Shiloh from Judd's abuse.

At the conclusion of the novel, Marty gains insight about why Judd is so mean, and he begins to treat Judd in a friendly manner. Marty keeps up his end of their bargain and realizes that "nothing is as simple as you guess . . ." He has matured and "opened [his] eyes some," understanding that everyone's approach to a problem or dilemma is different and his way may not have been the best, but it worked.

Dad (Ray Preston)

Marty's dad works hard at his job as a postal carrier. Family is important to Dad. Even though they don't have much money, they manage to send any extra money to his sister, Hettie, to help care for his ailing mother. Marty's father is a proud man who values truth and honesty. He understands the ways of the people who live in Tyler County. He respects other people and their privacy, he minds his own business, and he has "the sense to shut up"—qualities that he tries to impress upon Marty.

Marty's dad gets upset with Marty for speaking boldly to Judd Travers, but he seems to understand and is gentle with him. Dad always looks out for Marty. Knowing that Marty wants to find out how Shiloh is, Dad indirectly asks Judd questions about his dogs when he delivers Judd's mail. Marty is aware of Dad's consideration. Dad is perceptive; he notices that Marty is not acting like himself, and so he discusses

Marty's behavior with Ma. Dad is concerned about Marty. Dad is also quite sensitive. When the German shepherd attacks Shiloh, Dad takes Shiloh to Doc Murphy rather than back to Judd. Dad never yells at Marty or punishes him for telling lies and hiding Shiloh. Instead, he doesn't say anything, forcing Marty to accept responsibility for his actions and tell the truth. Dad also agrees to let Shiloh stay with them until Shiloh's wounds have healed. When Shiloh is staying in the Prestons' kitchen, even Dad becomes attached to the little dog and can be seen petting Shiloh and letting Shiloh lick his plate clean. Dad is patient and forgiving, seeming to understand Marty's dilemma about Shiloh.

Ma (Lou Preston)

Marty's ma has ". . . a pretty face. Plain, but smooth." She takes care of the house and children. When she can get outside work to do at home, such as stuffing envelopes, she does that to help out with their bills. Ma is observant and intuitive. She seems to know just what Marty is thinking most of the time. Ma discovers that Marty is hiding Shiloh. She is perceptive and realizes that Marty might run away with Shiloh. She is adamant when she tells Marty never to run away from a problem. In spite of her better judgment (because she has never kept a secret from Dad), she agrees not to tell Dad about Shiloh until the next day. Of course, when the German shepherd attacks Shiloh, and Dad finds out that Ma has known that Marty has been hiding Shiloh, he is upset with her for not telling him.

Ma is a caring person. She quickly grows attached to Shiloh and even bakes a cake to celebrate the last day Marty has to work for Judd and Shiloh becomes their dog.

Judd Travers

Judd Travers is a mean looking man who lives alone in a trailer not far from the Prestons. He has a "big round face, whiskers on his cheeks and chin where he hasn't shaved . . . tight little eyes . . . beneath big bushy brows." His teeth are stained from chewing tobacco and he has a noticeable belly. Judd reads *Guns and Ammo* and *Shooting Times* magazines. He shoots small game like rabbits and opossum and has been known to shoot deer out of season.

Judd is dishonest, crude, and insensitive. He abuses his dogs and thinks he is above the law. He tells Marty's father that the "law never told me before what I could do with my dogs, won't be tellin' me now." He talks about kicking his dogs and not feeding them when they've done something he dislikes.

Judd reveals to Marty that his father abused him as a child. Because no one ever felt sorry for him, he never felt sorry for anyone else. As a result of being abused, Judd is angry. He is unfamiliar with feelings related to kindness or friendliness. The closest Judd comes to showing any sensitivity at all is when he leaves a glass of water—with ice—for Marty when Marty is working for him. The last day Marty works for Judd, it is as though Judd really doesn't want to see Marty go because he will miss Marty's company. Marty paid attention to Judd and talked to him as though he mattered. Judd shows that when a person is treated with respect and someone pays attention to them, they can make changes. Underneath Judd's meanness, he shows that he can be decent. He acknowledges Shiloh by name and even gives Marty a collar for Shiloh.

David Howard

David is Marty's best friend. His life is not at all like Marty's. He lives in a big, two-story house in Friendly. His mother is a teacher and his father works for the *Tyler Star-News*. His mother makes fancy lunches for David and Marty and sits down to eat with them. (When David visits Marty's house, Marty's mother gives them a bag lunch and they go up on the hill to eat.) David always has different toys to play with and lives a privileged life in comparison to Marty's life. In spite of the differences in the way the two boys live, David and Marty are best friends. They seem to enjoy each other's company and their differences seem to complement each other.

Activities for Readers

1. Marty has never had a pet before Shiloh comes along. He quickly realizes that owning a pet involves responsibility. Using the library or the Internet, research pet care and pet ownership. What would you need to know about having a pet in order to be a responsible pet owner? List your findings.

2. Marty was determined to keep Shiloh. If Marty had not seen Judd shoot the deer, what would he have said to Judd? Rewrite the last three chapters of the novel as if Judd had not shot the deer.

3. Create a three-dimensional map of Marty's house, the woods and hills that surround his house, the pen he built for Shiloh, and the barn.

4. Write a persuasive letter to the editor of the local Friendly newspaper in which you support either more restrictive hunting laws or less restrictive hunting laws.

Additional Resources

Children's Literature Review. Vol. 17. Detroit: Gale Research, 1989: 48–62.

Contemporary Authors New Revision Series. Vol. 24. Detroit: Gale Research, 1988: 334–335.

Contemporary Authors New Revision Series. Vol. 8. Detroit: Gale Research, 1983: 380–381.

Naylor, Phyllis Reynolds. "Newbery Acceptance Speech." *The Horn Book Magazine.* July–August 1992: 404–411.

Naylor, Phyllis Reynolds. "Phyllis Reynolds Naylor." The Children's Book Guild of Washington, D.C., 1999. Online. www.childrens bookguild.org/PhyllisNaylor.html.

Naylor, Rex. "Phyllis Reynolds Naylor." *The Horn Book Magazine.* July–August 1992: 412–415.

"Phyllis Reynolds Naylor." *Random House.* Online. www.random house.com/teachersbdd/nayl.html.

"Phyllis Reynolds Naylor." *The Internet Public Library.* Online. www.ipl.org/youth/AskAuthor/Naylor.html.

Ruthven, Beverly and Rogers, Sue F. "Shiloh." *Beacham's Desktop Guide to Literature For Intermediate Students.* Florida: Beacham Publishing, Inc., 1995: 400–407.

MANIAC MAGEE (1991)

Life and Background of the Author

Jerry Spinelli's first published novel was *Space Station Seventh Grade* (1982). Since then, he has written over fifteen novels for adolescents, about adolescence. Spinelli's writing concerns controversial topics such as racism, sexism, and homelessness, while accurately and humorously depicting adolescents. At times, he has experienced parental objections because his stories are seemingly "too realistic." His young readers, however, relate to his characters and their dilemmas because they share similar experiences. Spinelli relies on memories of his own adolescence and the real-life events that have occurred in the lives of his six children to convey his views of the world to his audience.

Spinelli was born on February 1, 1941, in Norristown, Pennsylvania, to Lou Spinelli, a typesetter, and Lorna Bigler. His family lived in an apartment that was situated in front of a smelly brewery in the East End of Norristown. A few years later, his family moved a few streets away, to a house located just two doors away from his grandparents' house, and in 1945, his brother, Billy, was born. When Spinelli was six years old, his parents bought a house in the West End of Norristown, so they moved once more. They spent the next ten years in this house. Spinelli grew to love the neighborhood—it was home. When Spinelli wasn't in school, he spent time riding his bicycle, skimming stones across Stony Creek, flipping baseball cards, and running on the railroad tracks behind their house. Spinelli was always involved in one sport or another—he played basketball, track and field, football, and Little League baseball (he always wanted to be a major league baseball player).

Spinelli didn't read much as a child because he was always too busy playing sports. He reserved reading for times when he was "bored." He did, however, read comic books and had a subscription for Bugs Bunny comic books. He also read books by Clair Bee who wrote a series of books about Chip Hilton, a high school athlete.

When Spinelli was in the ninth grade, he felt as though he was on top of the world. He was class president, king of the ninth grade prom, and had a girlfriend. Everything changed when his family moved to a new house. He still attended the same school and had the same friends, but he no longer felt the same. The old neighborhood had been Spinelli's world for ten years, and he missed it terribly. Spinelli felt lost. That same year, Spinelli's high school football team won a big game. After the game, he went home and wrote a poem about the game. A few days later, his poem was published in the local newspaper. Spinelli gave up his dream of becoming a major league baseball player and decided he wanted to be a writer instead.

After graduating from high school, Spinelli attended Gettysburg College and received an A.B. degree in 1963 (an A.B., or Artium Baccalaureatus, is awarded to students who include significant coursework in the Classics in their curriculum of study). In 1964, he received his Master of Arts degree from Johns Hopkins University. Spinelli served in the Naval Reserve from 1966 until 1972. During 1966, he also began working for Chilton Company as a magazine editor. Spinelli worked as an editor until 1989, spending his lunch hours writing books for adults—none of which were published.

On May 21, 1977, Spinelli married Eileen Mesi who is also a writer. Spinelli became a father overnight because Eileen had six children. Spinelli gets many of his ideas for stories from his children who were always into something as they were growing up. He also gets ideas from everyday life and from memories he has of his own childhood and adolescence.

Spinelli has received numerous awards for his writing. *Maniac Magee* received the 1991 Newbery Medal, the Boston Globe-Horn Book Award (1990), the Notable Children's Books Award (ALA) (1991), the Best Books for Young Adults Award (ALA) (1991), and the Children's Editors' Choices Award (Booklist) (1990). *Wringer* was named Newbery Honor Book in 1998 and received the Notable Children's Books Award (ALA) (1998), the Horn Book Fanfare Award (1998), the Children's Editors' Choices Award (Booklist) (1997), and many other awards in 1997 and 1998.

Today, Spinelli lives in Phoenixville, Pennsylvania, with his wife Eileen. He writes in his office on the second floor of their house.

Spinelli's Selected Works

Space Station Seventh Grade (1982)

Who Put That Hair in My Toothbrush? (1984)

Night of the Whale (1985)

Jason and Marceline (1986)

Dump Days (1988)

The Bathwater Gang (1990)

Maniac Magee: A Novel (1990)

Book Cooks (1991)

Fourth Grade Rats (1991)

School Daze: Report to the Principal's Office (1991)

There's a Girl in My Hammerlock (1991)

The Bathwater Gang Gets Down to Business (1992)

Do the Funky Pickle (1992)

Who Ran My Underwear Up the Flagpole? (1992)

Picklemania (1993)

Tooter Pepperday (1995)

Crash (1996)

The Library Card (1997)

Wringer (1997)

Blue Ribbon Blues: A Tooter Tale (1998)

Knots in My Yo-Yo String: The Autobiography of a Kid (1998)

Stargirl (2000)

Spinelli has also been a contributor to books—*Our Roots Grow Deeper Than We Know: Pennsylvania Writers—Pennsylvania Life* (1995), edited by Lee Gutkind, and *Noble Pursuits* (1988), edited by Virginia A. Arnold and Carl B. Smith. His work has also been included in anthologies, such as *Best Sports Stories of 1982* and *Connections*, a book of short stories.

A Brief Synopsis

Maniac Magee is about Jeffrey Lionel Magee's search for "home" and the racial prejudice in the town of Two Mills. Spinelli has written the novel in third person ("He said," as opposed to "I said," which is called first person), using an objective viewpoint (in which the thoughts and feelings of the characters are not revealed).

Jeffrey lived in Bridgeport with his parents until he was three years old. During that year he became an orphan. His parents were killed in a trolley accident over the Schuylkill River. During the next eight years, Jeffrey lives with his Aunt Dot and Uncle Dan in Hollidaysburg, Pennsylvania. The household is extremely dysfunctional because his aunt and uncle never speak to each other. They dislike each other but, being strict Catholics, refuse to divorce. After being bounced back and forth between his aunt and uncle, Jeffrey reaches his breaking point. At the spring musical at Jeffrey's school (Jeffrey is in the chorus), which his aunt and uncle attend, he screams at the top of his lungs, "Talk! Talk! Talk!" and then runs away.

Jeffrey begins his search for a new home. He runs for a year, and with his sneakers falling apart, he ends up in Two Mills, a town linked to Bridgeport (the town he grew up in) by the Schuylkill Bridge. The first day he is in Two Mills, he makes four appearances. First, he speaks to a black girl, who appears to be close to his age, named Amanda Beale. She has a suitcase that he discovers is full of books. He borrows a book from her and promises to return it.

Jeffrey's second appearance is at the high school football field. He catches a pass meant for Hands Down, a receiver on the football team. After running all the way to the soccer field, he performs one of his amazing feats—he punts the football back to the football team, a punt that travels farther than any of the football players has ever thrown it, all the while holding onto his borrowed book. Next, he rescues a 10-year-old boy from Finsterwald's backyard, a place that causes terror in all the kids in West End, and then responds to Mrs. Pickwell's whistle when she calls all ten of her children home for dinner. He sits down to a spaghetti dinner with the large family without anyone asking any questions. The next time Jeffrey is noticed is at a Little League game. He again performs incredible feats by hitting John McNab's fastball and bunting a "frogball" for several home runs. Whenever anyone spots Jeffrey he is running—fast. Stories begin to circulate about Jeffrey's amazing feats earning him the nickname "Maniac."

Theme

Jeffrey learns that Two Mills is segregated—the East End is where the black people live and the West End is where the white people live, and the dividing line is Hector Street. After being chased by John McNab and his group of friends, the Cobras, Maniac ends up in the East End and is confronted for the first time by Mars Bar. Maniac is oblivious to the racial differences that exist between them. Rescued by Amanda Beale, Maniac goes to the Beale house. After revealing to Mr. Beale that his home is the deer shed at the zoo, the Beales invite Maniac to stay with them. He finally has a home with an address.

Maniac is happy with his life. He fits in with the Beales just like he belongs there; however, he is unaware of the prejudice that exists between the blacks in the East End and the whites in the West End until an old black man calls him "Whitey" and tells him to "go home." The situation escalates when graffiti is written on the side of the Beale house ("Fishbelly go home.") and when Amanda's coveted Volume A of the encyclopedia is stolen, cut up, and used as confetti when Maniac untangles Cobbles Knot. When he realizes that his presence in the Beale house is hurting the Beales, Maniac walks down the center of the street, between the blacks and the whites, out of town.

Character Insight

Maniac is found, hungry, scraped up, and dirty in the buffalo pen at the zoo by an old man named Grayson. Grayson takes him to the baseball equipment room in the band shell. He feeds Maniac, buys him some clothes, and lets him stay in the baseball room. Maniac and Grayson become close friends. As they get to know each other, Maniac finds out that Grayson played baseball in the minor leagues and doesn't know how to read. Maniac teaches Grayson how to read and Grayson teaches Maniac about baseball. Maniac also enlightens Grayson about black people, telling him that they are just like white people, a surprise to Grayson. Maniac and Grayson are happy together and once again, Maniac has a home with an address he makes up: 101 Band Shell Boulevard. They happily spend the Thanksgiving and Christmas holidays together, and five days after Christmas, Grayson dies in his sleep. Maniac is alone again. To deal with his grief, Maniac runs wherever his legs will take him.

Depressed and lonely, Maniac ends up at Valley Forge where he decides to die. He refuses to allow anyone else to orphan him. The second night Maniac is there in a small cabin, two small boys show up, Piper and Russell McNab, brothers of John McNab. The young boys are running away from home. Maniac takes the boys back to the McNab house and ends up staying there. The house is dirty and messy and has cockroaches crawling everywhere. Maniac performs "heroic feats," to persuade Piper and Russell to go to school.

Piper and Russell dare Maniac to go to the East End (they don't know he used to live there). Maniac uses the dare to get the boys to go to school. While walking through the East End, Maniac encounters

Mars Bar, who insists on racing him. A crowd gathers and they race. Maniac wins, beating Mars Bar and running the last few feet of the race backwards. Maniac regrets humiliating Mars Bar by running backwards; however, his actions cause Mars Bar to hate *him* (an individual) rather than white people in general.

At the McNab house, the Cobras (John McNab's group of friends) are building what they call a "pillbox" in the middle of the living room. The "pillbox" is a fortress to protect themselves against blacks. John envisions blacks from the East End attacking the West End all at once, probably in the summer. The idea of the fortress and the prejudicial attitude that prevails within the McNab household causes Maniac to feel dirty.

Maniac leaves the McNabs, choosing to sleep in the park. He couldn't stand what the McNabs were doing or the way they were thinking. Russell and Piper find him in the library and insist Maniac come to Piper's birthday party. Maniac agrees—as long as he can bring a friend. His idea is to bring Mars Bar and his intention is to teach the McNabs that blacks are human beings just like themselves, and to teach Mars Bar the same thing about whites.

Mars Bar accepts Maniac's challenge and courageously goes to the West End with Maniac. They go to the Pickwells' house to eat, and Mars Bar is readily accepted by the entire family. Then they go to the McNabs' house, where John and the Cobras try to intimidate Mars Bar. Maniac has to drag Mars Bar out of the house to prevent a fight from erupting. Mars Bar asks Maniac, "Wha'd you think?" When they part, Mars Bar is angry with Maniac.

Eventually, Maniac and Mars Bar begin to run together in the mornings and learn to respect each other. Mars Bar rescues Russell McNab from the trolley trestle (the site of Maniac's parents' death) and takes him home—to the West End. In his way, Maniac succeeds in breaking down barriers between blacks and whites. Mars Bar and Amanda find Maniac in the buffalo pen at the zoo and insist that he return to the Beales'. Maniac finally feels as though he is going home.

Character Map

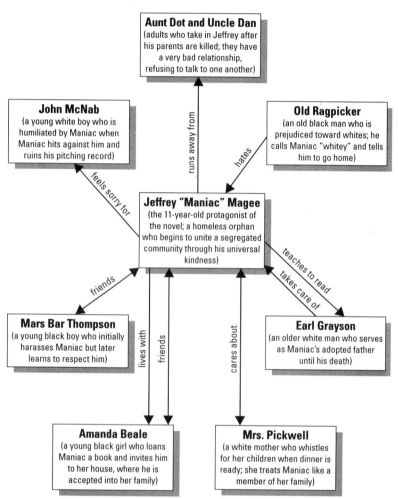

Aunt Dot and Uncle Dan
(adults who take in Jeffrey after his parents are killed; they have a very bad relationship, refusing to talk to one another)

John McNab
(a young white boy who is humiliated by Maniac when Maniac hits against him and ruins his pitching record)

Old Ragpicker
(an old black man who is prejudiced toward whites; he calls Maniac "whitey" and tells him to go home)

runs away from

hates

feels sorry for

Jeffrey "Maniac" Magee
(the 11-year-old protagonist of the novel; a homeless orphan who begins to unite a segregated community through his universal kindness)

teaches to read

takes care of

friends

Mars Bar Thompson
(a young black boy who initially harasses Maniac but later learns to respect him)

Earl Grayson
(an older white man who serves as Maniac's adopted father until his death)

lives with

friends

cares about

Amanda Beale
(a young black girl who loans Maniac a book and invites him to her house, where he is accepted into her family)

Mrs. Pickwell
(a white mother who whistles for her children when dinner is ready; she treats Maniac like a member of her family)

Major Themes

In this novel of a young boy's attempt to unify the town of Two Mills, Spinelli juxtaposes three distinct themes: homelessness, racial prejudice, and literacy. The themes demonstrate Spinelli's realistic portrayal of the world as he sees it.

Literary
Device

Throughout the novel, Spinelli focuses on home—or the lack of it. Maniac "was not born in a dump." In fact, the first three years of his life were spent in an average house with a mother and father. He has a home and a family—a place where he belonged. When his parents are killed, his home and family cease to exist. He lives with his Aunt Dot and Uncle Dan. Even though he lives in a house, he does not feel as though he belongs or as though he is "home." At the age of 11, Maniac chooses homelessness over a dysfunctional household.

Theme

Spinelli reinforces the significance of having a home—an address—when he says that Maniac, the legend, has a name, but not an official address with numbers. Maniac lives in the deer shed at the zoo. When Maniac is running from John McNab and the Cobras, he sees "the town whizzing past . . . a blur of faces, each face staring from its own window, each face in its own personal frame, its own house, its own address, someplace to be when there was no other place to be, how lucky to be a face staring out from a window. . . ." Maniac soon discovers a home for himself at the Beales and is happy to have an address. Despite the fact that the Beales are black and Maniac is white, he fits in and loves his new home. For a change, *he* is on the inside.

Character
Insight

Because Maniac is homeless before living with the Beales, he knows how to survive on the streets. His notion of survival is a harsh contrast to the "cardinal rules of survival in the West End." which are simply to stay away from Finsterwald's and from high school boys. After experiencing racial discrimination, Maniac thinks he should leave the Beales because his presence is bringing them pain. He frustrates Amanda by refuting her argument about why he should stay at the Beales with his own argument about how he can survive on the streets. Maniac's feelings are hurt when Amanda tells him that he "*can't* get a library card without an *address!*"

Theme

Living in the band shell, Maniac has an address again—101 Band Shell Boulevard—and a family in the form of Earl Grayson. Maniac doesn't attend school because to him, "school seems sort of like a big home, but only a day home. . . ." Maniac feels that, because you can't live in a school, you would need a night home with an address, a place "where everybody talks to each other and uses the same toaster" (in contrast to his aunt and uncle's house). Having a day home without having a night home doesn't make sense to Maniac.

When Grayson dies, Maniac is once again without a home and a family. He ends up staying at the McNabs' house, wondering why he is there. It is a roof over his head, but it isn't a *home* or a *family*. After Maniac manipulates Mars Bar into going to the McNabs', he walks around until he thinks he should go home—only to sadly remember that he doesn't have a home.

Maniac is found by Mars Bar and Amanda as he is sleeping once again in the buffalo pen at the zoo. Amanda insists that Maniac "come home." At long last, Maniac "knew that finally, truly, at long last, someone was calling him home."

Theme

Racial prejudice is another major theme of *Maniac Magee*. When Maniac jogs into Two Mills, he says "hi" to everyone he passes. The people are taken aback because "people just didn't say that to strangers, out of the blue." Spinelli suggests that people in today's society are alienated from one another and are strangers to each other, particularly along racial lines.

Literary Device

In Two Mills, the racial line, or boundary, between the blacks and whites is Hector Street. The blacks live in the East End and the whites live in the West End. Spinelli uses Maniac as a catalyst to unite the East End and the West End. When Maniac meets Amanda Beale, a black girl, she is suspicious of him. She wonders what a white kid is doing in the East End. Maniac is oblivious to the difference in their skin color. He and Amanda share an interest in books and become friends. Maniac lives with the Beales and is accepted as part of the family. The image of Maniac taking a bath with Hester and Lester Beale portrays the joining of the races to live together as family and Spinelli's ultimate hope for desegregation and an end to racial prejudice.

The color of someone's skin is not a problem for Maniac. He loves the colors of the people in the East End. He "[can't] see it, this color business." Nor does he see the dislike and hatred that is directed at him because he is white. He is called "whitey" by the old ragpicker, "fish-belly" by Mars Bar, and a racial epithet is scrawled on the Beale's house attacking Maniac because he is not black.

Spinelli portrays the ignorance people have about races different from their own. Maniac is harassed by Mars Bar and does the unthinkable—he takes a bite of Mars Bar's candy, biting over the exact spot where Mars Bar had bitten. It is as though "black germs" or "white germs" are deadly to the opposite race. Maniac educates Grayson about blacks, explaining to him that they are "regular people, like us." Similarly, the McNabs do not understand blacks. The McNabs believe blacks are "today's Indians" who are going to revolt and attack whites.

When Maniac races Mars Bar, and shows him up, Mars Bar's hatred towards whites becomes a hatred for one person: Maniac. Mars Bar is able to rise above race and see Maniac as a human being. This change in Mars Bar allows Maniac and Mars Bar to develop respect for each other and later, a trusting friendship.

Maniac tries to perform a "miracle" by taking Mars Bar to the McNab house. He realizes that the unification, or desegregation, of Two Mills will have to be accomplished by educating people about the opposite race. Even though Maniac's plan is not totally successful, it paves the way for better relations along Hector Street.

Literacy is the third significant theme that Spinelli addresses in *Maniac Magee*. Reading and learning is exhibited throughout the novel as something positive and good. Amanda Beale carries all of her books—her prized possessions—with her at all times in a suitcase so they will not be ruined by her younger siblings or dog. Maniac carries a book with him wherever he goes when he first arrives in Two Mills. When he is living with the Beales, he reads to Hester and Lester. Spinelli includes the destruction of Amanda's Volume A of the encyclopedia and portrays it as a tragedy. Later, living with Grayson, Maniac begins his own library, buying books about a variety of topics from the library. He tells Grayson that he wants all the books he can get because he's "learning everything!" Maniac even teaches Grayson to read and when Grayson reads his first book cover to cover, the accomplishment is worthy of a celebration.

Exposing his readers to the issues of homelessness, racial prejudice and discrimination, and the importance of literacy, Spinelli attempts to instill hope and enthusiasm for a society of more tolerant and understanding human beings.

About the Characters

Jeffrey Lionel (Maniac) Magee

Maniac is an 11-year-old homeless orphan. After imparting the "birth scream of a legend" during his elementary school concert, Maniac runs from the dysfunctional home of his Aunt Dot and Uncle Dan. He shows up in Two Mills, "a scraggly little kid jogging . . . the soles of both sneakers hanging by their hinges and flopping open. . . ." He is friendly and open minded, saying "hi" to everyone he passes and ignoring the prejudice that exists in Two Mills.

In Maniac Magee, Spinelli has created a legendary character. When Maniac arrives in Two Mills, he performs extraordinary feats that amaze everyone, making him "cool times ten." With a book in one hand, he catches a football and punts it perfectly. Unafraid, he rescues a young boy from Finsterwald's yard. John McNab, a Little League pitcher who throws fastballs, does not intimidate Maniac. Maniac hits several home runs—breaking John's perfect record. Maniac also runs on the rails of the railroad track, and when he wanders—which he does often—he jogs. Maniac's reputation precedes him wherever he goes in Two Mills. Even though the feats that he performs make him "different" from others, Maniac appears unaffected by his talents.

Maniac makes a "home" for himself in the deer pen at the zoo. He never complains about his homelessness; however, his embarrassment and shame are evident when Mr. Beale drives him "home." Maniac gives Mr. Beale an address in the East End, an unrealistic address because only black people live in the East End. He is somewhat naïve because he is "blind" to the dividing line, Hector Street, which separates the East End where the blacks live and the West End where the whites live.

Maniac is a catalyst used by Spinelli to try to unite the East End and the West End. Maniac is oblivious to discrimination and prejudice. The Beales, a black family, invite him to live with them. Maniac loves his life with the Beales and "can't see this color business." Color means nothing to Maniac. "For the life of him he [can't] figure out why . . . East Enders call[ed] themselves black." He observes a variety of colors in the East End, but not black. Maniac is also unaware of the negative feelings each race has for the other. Consequently, he is unprepared when Mars Bar tries to intimidate and hurt him or when John McNab and the Cobras chase him into the East End and stand on Hector Street laughing at him. Maniac is perceptive, and soon realizes that what he is experiencing is discrimination. He is called "whitey," "honkeydonkey," and "fishbelly." When a racial epithet is written on the Beales' house, Maniac realizes that his presence is causing them pain, so he gives up his new home.

Maniac educates Grayson and the McNabs about black people, and he educates Mars Bar about white people. He realizes that prejudice and discrimination stem from ignorance.

Maniac has "bad luck with parents." His own parents were killed when he was three years old, he feels he has to protect the Beales, so he leaves their home; Grayson, who cares for him as his own child, dies. Maniac's response to his grief and despair is to run. Running relieves Maniac's pain. When Maniac can't alleviate his pain by running, he attempts to commit suicide; however, his compassion for others (runaways Russell and Piper McNab) does not allow him to take his life.

Throughout the novel, Maniac's love for books and learning is evident. Even though he doesn't attend school, he understands the importance of it. He borrows a book from Amanda Beale, buys books from the library, teaches Grayson to read, and performs amazing feats to bribe Russell and Piper to go to school.

Maniac's goal is to have a home—an address—a place to go where people love and talk to each other. He is proud of his address when he first lives with the Beales. When he lives with Grayson, and feels as though he is "home," he makes up an address for the band shell. And finally when Amanda takes him back to the Beales', Maniac knows that finally "someone was calling him home."

Amada Beale

Amanda Beale is a young black girl who attends elementary school in the East End. She has a small library of books that she is "finicky about." To prevent her brother, sister, and dog from ruining her books, she carries them to school everyday in a suitcase. Her most prized possession is her Volume A of an encyclopedia.

Amanda is a friendly and generous person. Even though she is suspicious of Maniac, a white stranger, she loans him one of her books and later defends him and invites him to her home. She gives up her room so Maniac can live with her family and she shares her books with him.

Like Maniac, Amanda is not prejudiced towards the opposite race. She loves him as a brother despite his white skin color. Amanda tries to protect Maniac from the cruelty of discrimination by preventing him from seeing the racial epithet that is written on the side of the Beales' house. She is hurt when Maniac leaves. At the conclusion of the novel, Amanda accompanies Mars Bar to the zoo (where Maniac is sleeping) to urge Maniac to return to the Beales' house to live. She tells Maniac that he is going home with her and he is "going to sleep there tonight and *tomorrow* night and the night after *that* and *every* night. . . ."

John McNab

John McNab is a "giant." He is five feet eight inches tall, weighs one hundred and seventy pounds, and is only 12 years old. He pitches for one of the Little League teams in Two Mills. He is "like a shark," because he strikes out all of the players on the opposing team with his fastball. When Maniac arrives in Two Mills, not only does he hit McNab's fast ball, but he hits home runs and humiliates McNab. To retaliate, McNab and his group of friends (they call themselves the Cobras) chase Maniac into the East End. McNab and the Cobras stop at Hector Street, the dividing line between West End where the whites live, and East End where the blacks live. They laugh, believing they have inflicted the worst possible punishment on Maniac.

Later in the novel, when Maniac returns Russell and Piper (John's younger brothers) to the McNab household, John is grateful. Maniac ends up staying at the McNabs' even though it is a chaotic and filthy environment. Maniac meets John's father and feels uneasy because John's father appears to be a racist. He also observes the McNabs and the Cobras building a fortress (a "pillbox") out of cement blocks—in the living room of the house. The fortress is a defense against "today's Indians," the blacks, when they revolt. Because of John's ignorance of black people and his father's racist influence, he is prejudiced toward black people.

When Maniac brings Mars Bar to the McNab house for Piper's birthday party, John attempts to intimidate Mars Bar and cause Mars Bar to initiate a fight. Maniac intercedes and Mars Bar criticizes the disgusting condition of the McNab house. Because Maniac defends Mars Bar, and because Maniac is viewed as a hero in Two Mills, it is logical to assume that after the interaction between John and Mars Bar, John views black people differently. However, Spinelli does not reveal any changes that take place regarding John's attitude toward black people; this issue is left to the reader to decide.

Mars Bar Thompson

Mars Bar Thompson is a young black boy who lives in the East End. He is a dynamic character. He changes during the course of the novel due to his experiences and actions. At first, Spinelli describes Mars Bar as a stereotypical tough-acting, not-afraid-of-anything bully. Mars Bar harasses Maniac by blocking his way and tries to intimidate Maniac with an intense glare. Mars Bar uses words spoken in the East End such as "bad" and "fishbelly." Mars Bar walks with a "super-slow dip-stride slumpshuffle," which is said to stop traffic because it takes him so long to cross the street.

Mars Bar dislikes Maniac because Maniac is white. Maniac confuses him because Maniac is not prejudiced toward him or afraid of him. When Maniac takes a bite of Mars Bar's candy—an unheard of act because blacks and whites never put their mouths where the other has been—Mars Bar is shocked by Maniac's nerve. Later, Spinelli implies that Mars Bar put the racial epithet on the Beales' house because he'd previously called Maniac "fishbelly" and because he is prejudiced against whites. As Maniac leaves town, Mars Bar and his group of friends heckle him.

Mars Bar is as ignorant of white people as John McNab is of black people. Mars Bar challenges Maniac to a race and loses. Because Maniac humiliates him by showing him up, Mars Bars' hatred is directed at Maniac rather than at the white race. Mars Bar begins to change when he can finally see Maniac as an individual. Afterward, when Maniac goads Mars Bar into being the "baddest" by crossing Hector Street and going to the West End, Mars Bar feels proud because his fame has spread to the West End. The Pickwell children know who he is and are respectful of him. The McNabs, on the other hand, are disrespectful. While Mars Bar is at the McNab house, Mars Bar is quite uncomfortable. "His jaw [is] clenched and his eyes [keep] straying to the gaping hole in the ceiling—and to the Cobras. . . ." Mars Bar is "as scared as any normal kid would be, but [is] not showing it . . ." Underneath Mars Bar's bravado, he is vulnerable just like anyone else. Crossing Hector Street with Maniac earns him Maniac's respect—not for what he does, but for the person he is.

Mars Bar begins running in the early mornings like Maniac. Soon they are running together, never talking or paying attention to the other. Mars Bar and Maniac become equals. Mars Bar forgets color, rescues Russell McNab from the trolley trestle, and takes the McNab brothers back home—to the West End. Mars Bar shows his concern and love for Maniac when he finds him sleeping in the buffalo pen at the zoo. Mars Bar even invites Maniac to live with him and his family. Spinelli creates the friendship between Mars Bar and Maniac to portray the beginning of desegregation in Two Mills.

Grayson

Earl Grayson is a "grizzled" old man who finds Maniac at the zoo. Grayson takes Maniac to the band shell and feeds and clothes him. As Grayson and Maniac get to know each other, a devoted friendship develops between them. Grayson tells Maniac stories of having been a pitcher for a minor league baseball team and gives maniac his old baseball glove for Christmas. Grayson is embarrassed when he admits to Maniac that he is illiterate—he can't read or write. Because he trusts Maniac, he asks Maniac to teach him to read.

Grayson is also a character who is ignorant about black people. He asks Maniac questions about the Beales, and when Maniac tells him that, "they're just regular people like us," Grayson responds, in disbelief, "ain't that somethin'. . . ."

After Grayson reads his first book cover to cover, Maniac hugs him. Grayson feels "unburdened for the first time in thirty-seven years. . . ." He feels loved by Maniac, as a son would love his father.

Grayson and Maniac are two misfits who, as fate would have it, find each other. They bring out the best in each other and, due to the nurturing each provides the other, they shine and are happy with the nontraditional family they create. Grayson dies a happy man.

Activities for Readers

1. In Chapter 44, Mars Bar rescues Russell McNab from the trolley trestle as Maniac runs away. What would have happened if Mars Bar had not been with Maniac? Rewrite the incident from this perspective.

2. During the novel, Maniac is homeless at different times. Using community resources, research the homeless population where you live. What can be done to assist the homeless in your area?

3. Choose one of the main characters—Maniac, Amanda, Mars Bar, or John McNab—and write about the character's life as you imagine it will be five years after the story ends.

4. What would it take to desegregate Two Mills? Write a letter to a congressman of Two Mills telling why Two Mills ought to be desegregated. Outline your plan for desegregation.

Additional Resources

Children's Literature Review. Vol. 26. Detroit: Gale Research, 1992: 201–207.

Contemporary Authors New Revision Series. Vol. 30. Detroit: Gale Research, 1990: 424.

"Jerry Spinelli Interview Transcript." *Scholastic.* Online. teacher. scholastic.com/authorsandbooks/spinelli/tscript. htm.

"Jerry Spinelli's Biography." *Scholastic.* Online. teacher.scholastic. com/authorsandbooks/authors/spinelli/bio.htm.

"Jerry Spinelli." Reading Corner. Online. www.carr.lib.md.us/ authco/spinelli-j.htm.

Keller, John. "Jerry Spinelli." *The Horn Book Magazine.* July–August 1991: 433–436.

"Maniac Magee." Carol Hurst's Children's Literature Site. Online. www.carolhurst.com/titles/maniacmagee.html.

"Spinelli, Jerry." Educational Paperback Association. Online. www. edupaperback.org/authorbios/spinell.html.

Spinelli, Jerry. "Newbery Medal Acceptance." *The Horn Book Magazine.* July–August 1991: 426–432.

Spinelli, Jerry. *Knots in My Yo-Yo String: The Autobiography of a Kid.* New York: Alfred A. Knopf, 1998.

NUMBER THE STARS (1990)

Life and Background of the Author

Lois Lowry is a prolific writer. Since her first book, *A Summer to Die*, was published in 1977, she has written over twenty novels for young adults and has won numerous awards. Her writing style varies from the lighthearted, humorous Anastasia books to the much more serious issues (evident in Lowry's two Newbery Medal winners, *Number the Stars* and *The Giver*) that are a part of the adult world young people are preparing to enter. Her books portray sensitive, intelligent, witty protagonists faced with challenges and choices. Lowry writes about life transitions, the importance of family, true friendship, and the need for caring relationships between all human beings despite their differences.

Lowry was born in Honolulu, Hawaii, on March 20, 1937, to Robert E. Hammersberg, a United States Army dentist, and Katherine Landis Hammersberg. Because her father was a career Army officer, Lowry often moved during her childhood. Leaving Hawaii, her family moved to New York, and, in 1942 Lowry began kindergarten in a private school. She remembers wearing dog tags (identification tags) on a gold chain around her neck that were similar to the dog tags worn by her father. When her father was sent overseas, where he was stationed during most of World War II, her mother took Lowry and her older sister, Helen, to Pennsylvania to live with her family. During this time in Pennsylvania, Lowry's grandfather showered her with attention and affection, but her step-grandmother merely tolerated her. Because Lowry was a shy, introverted child, she sought companionship and entertainment in the wonderful worlds that existed within the books she found in her grandfather's library. While Lowry's father was overseas, her mother had a baby boy, named Jon, whom Lowry loved having in the house. After the war, Lowry and her family joined her father in Tokyo, Japan, where they lived for two years in an Americanized community.

At the outbreak of the Korean War in 1950, Lowry returned to the United States to attend a small, private high school in New York City. She had just turned 17 years old when she graduated from high school in a class of close to fifty students. The caption under her senior picture in the school yearbook reads, "Future Novelist." The following fall, Lowry entered Pembroke College, a branch of Brown University, in Rhode Island, to pursue her childhood dream of becoming a writer. However, she dropped out at the end of her sophomore year to get married at the age of 19. Because her husband, Donald Lowry, was a Naval officer, Lowry resumed a military lifestyle that included traveling and living wherever her husband was stationed. When her husband left the service to attend Harvard Law School, they settled in Cambridge, Massachusetts. After her husband finished law school, the Lowry family, which now included four children, moved to Portland, Maine. Lowry eventually received a bachelor's degree in 1973, at the age of 36, from the University of Southern Maine, and then immediately began work on a master's degree.

While attending graduate school, Lowry established herself as an accomplished freelance journalist. She began writing stories and articles that appeared in publications such as *Redbook*, *Yankee*, and *Down East*, as well as in newspapers. She also edited two textbooks—*Black American Literature* (1973) and *Literature of the American Revolution* (1974), both written by J. Weston Walsh—and became a photographer, specializing in photographs of children. In 1978, a collection of her photographs of buildings and houses was published in a book titled *Here in Kennebunkport*.

Lowry's first novel, *A Summer to Die* (1977), is about the relationship between two adolescent sisters, Meg and Molly, and the effect that Molly's death, as a result of leukemia, has on the family. Lowry based the relationship between Meg and Molly on her own memories of her relationship with her older sister, Helen, as they were growing up, and on the feelings and emotions that she felt when Helen died at the age of twenty-eight of cancer. Lowry experienced other heartaches as well. Lowry's oldest son, Grey, a fighter pilot in the United States Air Force, was killed in a plane crash in 1995. In addition, Lowry has a daughter who became disabled as a result of a disease involving the central nervous system. Her daughter's disability has reinforced Lowry's belief that people are "connected" despite their physical differences.

In 1977, Lowry and her husband divorced, and Lowry remained in Maine for the next two years, continuing to write. After completing another serious novel, *Find a Stranger, Say Goodbye* (1978), Lowry moved to Boston. Because she had been writing about serious and sad issues, she decided to write a humorous short story about a 10-year-old girl named Anastasia Krupnik. Anastasia is a gangly girl who wears glasses, has messy blonde hair, and is always getting into mischief. Lowry liked Anastasia and her family so much that the short story became the first chapter of her novel *Anastasia Krupnik* (1979), the first in a series of novels about Anastasia.

Lowry lives in Cambridge, Massachusetts and spends most weekends at her nineteenth-century farmhouse in New Hampshire. She spends at least five hours writing every single morning, working on more than one project at a time. When she isn't writing, she likes to cook, garden in the summer, and knit in the winter. She enjoys reading memoirs and biographies, taking exotic, adventurous trips, and going to as many movies as possible. She is also an accomplished photographer. The photograph of a young Swedish girl on the cover of the Yearling-Newbery edition of *Number the Stars* was taken by Lowry.

Lowry's novels cover a variety of topics that range in tone from serious to humorous and share many of the same themes: freedom, friendship, and the interdependency that exists between people. Through her writing, Lowry communicates her hope for human decency to exist in the world.

Lowry's Selected Works

Novels

A Summer to Die (1977)

Find a Stranger, Say Goodbye (1978)

Here in Kennebunkport (1978)

Anastasia Krupnik (1979)

Autumn Street (1980)

Anastasia Again! (1981)

Anastasia at Your Service (1982)

The One Hundredth Thing About Caroline (1983)

Taking Care of Terrific (1983)

Us and Uncle Fraud (1984)

Anastasia, Ask Your Analyst (1984)

Switcharound (1985)

Anastasia on Her Own (1985)

Anastasia Has the Answers (1986)

Rabble Starkey (1987)

Anastasia's Chosen Career (1987)

All About Sam (1988)

Number the Stars (1989)

Your Move, J.P.! (1990)

Anastasia at This Address (1991)

Attaboy, Sam! (1992)

The Giver (1993)

Anastasia, Absolutely (1995)

See You Around, Sam! (1996)

Stay! Keeper's Story (1997)

Looking Back: A Book of Memories (1998)

Zooman Sam (1999)

Gathering Blue (2000)

Short Stories

"Crow Call." (*Redbook*. December 1975)

"Splendor," *Short Takes: A Short Story Collection for Young Readers.* (Elizabeth Segal, editor, 1986)

"The Harringtons' Daughter," *A Gathering of Flowers: Stories about Being Young in America.* (Joyce Carol Thomas, editor, 1990)

"The Tree House," *The Big Book for Peace.* (Ann Durrell and Marily Sachs, editors, 1990)

"Elliot's House," *The Big Book for Our Planet.* (Ann Durrell, Jean Craighead George, and Katherine Paterson, editors, 1993)

"Holding," *Am I Blue?: Coming Out from the Silence.* (Marion Dane Bauer, editor, 1994)

A Brief Synopsis

Literary
Device

Number the Stars is a historical novel set in Denmark during World
War II. Lowry has written the novel in third person ("He says," as
opposed to, "I said," which is first person), using a limited omniscient
viewpoint (only Annemarie's thoughts and feelings are revealed). Ten-
year-old Annemarie Johansen and her family live in Copenhagen, Denmark. Their lives have changed drastically because the Nazis now
occupy Denmark (1943). Through Annemarie, we learn that the
Danes must abide by curfews and use blackout curtains on their windows. They have no fuel for heat, and electricity has been rationed.
The Danes must use candles to light their homes. They have sadly
become accustomed to Nazi soldiers standing on every street corner
and have learned to be "just another face in the crowd," going about
their business, trying not to be noticed by the Nazis. The adults are
fearful and sad because they understand the dangers of the Nazis occupation of Denmark and they have experienced loss resulting from the
actions of the Nazis. Annemarie's older sister, Lise, was killed because
she was an active member of the Danish Resistance, a group of people
opposed to the Nazi occupation of Denmark and supportive of the
Danish Jews. Annemarie, her five-year-old sister, Kirsti, and her best
friend, Ellen Rosen, are unaware of the danger that surrounds them.
They are only aware of obvious changes that have affected their lives.
They are aware of the food shortages (sugar is no longer available, they
eat bread without butter, and their mothers drink "coffee," which is
really just herb-flavored water); they can't get rubber tires so bicycles
have wooden wheels; they are unable to get leather shoes—just shoes
made from fish scales; and they play with paper dolls cut from old magazines. Some things, however, continue as usual. Annemarie still plays
with Ellen, and all of the children attend school. Annemarie's father
and Ellen's father go to work the same as always.

Literary
Device

Number the Stars begins with a foreboding tone. Annemarie, her sister, Kirsti, and Ellen are running home from school and are questioned
by the Nazi soldiers. Mrs. Hirsch, the button store owner, and her son
are taken away by the Nazis. When the Rosens, upstairs neighbors and
good friends of the Johansens, go to their synagogue to celebrate the
Jewish New Year, their rabbi warns them that they are in extreme danger of being taken and "relocated" by the Nazis. When the Johansens
find out, they offer to help them because, "that's what friends do."

The Rosens must go into hiding or risk being relocated by the Nazis. Peter Neilsen, Lise's fiancé and a member of the Resistance, takes Ellen's parents with him on the eve of the Jewish New Year. Ellen stays with Annemarie and her family pretending to be Annemarie's sister. The tone is suspenseful as Nazi soldiers demand entrance to the Johansens' apartment in the middle of the night, searching for the Rosens. Terrified, Annemarie notices that Ellen has on her Star of David necklace. Annemarie yanks the necklace from Ellen's neck and hides it in her hand. Because Ellen has dark hair and Annemarie and Kirsti have blonde hair, the soldiers question Annemarie's father about Ellen's identity. He corroborates Ellen's story, telling the soldiers that she is Lise. Mr. Johansen produces a picture of his dead daughter, Lise, who had dark hair as an infant. The soldiers reluctantly accept the picture as proof and before they leave the apartment, they spitefully destroy the pictures.

The next day, Mrs. Johansen takes Annemarie, Kirsti, and Ellen to her brother's farmhouse which is in Gilleleje, near the coast. Annemarie knows the trip is not a vacation, but she doesn't understand what is going on. The night before, when her parents telephoned her uncle, they seemed to be talking in code. They talked about "good days for fishing" and transporting cigarettes. Although Annemarie knows her Uncle Henrik, is a fisherman, she doesn't know that he has been transporting Danish Jews to neutral Sweden by hiding them in a secret hollowed out area in the bottom of his boat.

The trip to Uncle Henrik's is extremely dangerous. On the train, the Nazis question Mrs. Johansen and when Kirsti starts to talk to the soldiers, they fear she will innocently reveal that Ellen is Jewish. At Uncle Henrik's, Annemarie is told that her Great-aunt Birte has died and that people are going to gather at the house to pay their final respects. Annemarie is confused because she doesn't have a Great-aunt Birte. A casket arrives at the farmhouse and soon after, strangers gather at the house and sit near the casket. Peter Neilsen arrives with Ellen's parents. Annemarie realizes that all of the people are Jews. Nazi soldiers arrive and question Annemarie about the contents of the casket. She bravely tells them that her Great-aunt Birte has died. She understands how dangerous the situation is and soon learns that her Uncle Henrik is going to smuggle the Jews across the sea to Sweden. The casket is full of blankets and warm clothing for the Jews to take on their journey.

Character Insight

The Jews make it safely to the boat; however, Mr. Rosen has dropped an important envelope that was from Peter to Uncle Henrik. The situation becomes complicated when Mrs. Johansen, who led half of the Jews to Uncle Henrik's boat, breaks her ankle on her way back to the farmhouse. The only person left to take the envelope to Uncle Henrik is Annemarie. Instructed by her mother, she puts the envelope in the bottom of a basket, puts food on top of it, and then rushes off to catch the boat before it leaves the dock. On her way to the boat, she has to take a path through the woods. She thinks about the story of "Little Red Riding Hood," in an attempt to maintain her courage. Annemarie encounters Nazi soldiers with dogs. She is scared, but remembers how her little sister, Kirsti, acted one day when Nazi soldiers stopped them. She acted impatient and angry. Determined to get the envelope to Uncle Henrik, Annemarie acts the same way. The soldiers let her go, and Annemarie makes it to the boat. She is able to give Uncle Henrik the envelope that contains a handkerchief. The handkerchief has a chemical on it that causes the Nazis' dogs to lose their sense of smell temporarily. After sniffing the handkerchief, the dogs are unable to smell Uncle Henrik's hidden "cargo"—the Jewish people who he is smuggling to safety.

Theme

The Rosens and the other Jews make it safely to Sweden. Two years later, when the war is over, Annemarie asks her father to repair Ellen's Star of David Necklace that she has kept hidden. She puts it on and intends to wear it herself until the Rosens return home and she can give it back to her friend, Ellen.

Character Map

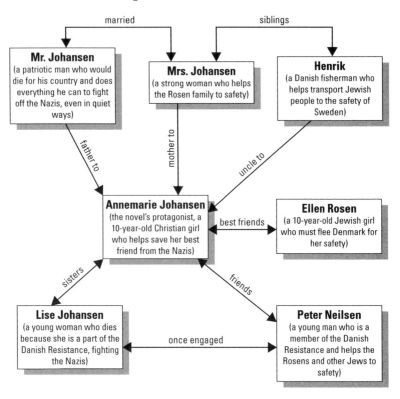

Geography

Major Themes

Theme

   Number the Stars explores the themes of bravery and true friend-ship. Lowry relies on historical accounts of actual events, her friend Annelise Platt's firsthand account of living in Denmark as a child dur-ing World War II, and her own determination and skill as a writer to relate her thematic messages.

   In the novel, bravery centers on individuals as well as the heroism of the entire nation of Denmark. Denmark, a small nation, was unable to defend itself against the Germans, so the King surrendered. How-ever, neither the people nor the King gave up. They sank their own naval ships to keep them from the Germans and they smuggled almost seven thousand Jews across the sea to Sweden. Even though the Danes could not fight the Germans as a unified nation, they showed their bravery with individual courageous acts—saving the Jews "one by one."

Character Insight

   Annemarie, the protagonist of the *Number the Stars*, learns the real meaning of bravery. Initially, she is unsure whether she will have the nerve to stand up for what she believes to be right. She thinks that ordinary people aren't called upon to be heroic, so she has nothing to worry about. When she is told that her friend Ellen and Ellen's par-ents are going to be "relocated" by the Nazi soldiers, she helps them escape from Denmark, risking her life a number of times. Annemarie discovers that ordinary people, like herself, can be brave when they are called to do so. She learns from her Uncle Henrik that "it is much *eas-ier* to be brave if you do not know everything," that even brave peo-ple are frightened, and if you are determined to stand up for what you believe, you don't consider the dangers.

   Other individuals who exhibit acts of bravery are Annemarie's parents and sister, Kirsti. Mr. and Mrs. Johansen are confronted with the Nazi soldiers several times. First, in their apartment when they are hiding Ellen, and again when they are on the train going to Gilleleje, and yet again at Uncle Henrik's during the gathering to pay respects to Annemarie's "Great-aunt Birte." They ignore the dangers and do what is necessary to protect Ellen and the other Jews. In her innocent manner, Kirsti is brave. She is fearless when confronted by the Nazi soldiers because she is too young to understand the threat of the political situation. Her obstinacy and talkative nature provide a role model for Annemarie when she is confronted in the woods by the Nazi soldiers. Peter Neilsen is also a courageous character, as was his fiancé, Lise. Both young people were members of the Danish Resistance. They fight injustice and work to get the Jews to safety. Both young people die for what they believe is right. Uncle Henrik, also a member of the Resistance, is a hero, too. Using his boat, he risks his life taking Jews to neutral Sweden.

Theme

True friendship is another major theme of *Number the Stars*. The Johansen family has a close friendship with the Rosen family. When the Rosens tell the Johansens that they have to go into hiding, the Johansens do not hesitate to offer their assistance because, "that's what friends do." The Johansen family risks their lives for their friends.

Character Insight

Despite the Nazi rule forbidding friendship between Jews and Christians, Annemarie and Ellen are best friends. Lowry portrays the characters as physical opposites—Annemarie is lanky and has blonde hair and Ellen is stocky and has dark hair—however, they enjoy each other's company immensely. In the beginning of the novel, when the Nazi soldiers confront the girls for the first time, it is clear that their friendship will be tested. Annemarie first proves her friendship for Ellen by yanking Ellen's Star of David necklace from her neck and hiding it in her hand so the German soldiers won't see it. Later, she risks her life when she takes the envelope that Mr. Rosen dropped to Uncle Henrik aboard his boat. All alone, she takes a path through the woods and is confronted by the Nazi soldiers. By acting like her younger sister, she is able to get the envelope with the handkerchief to Uncle Henrik. The Rosens and other Jews make it to Sweden and safety. Annemarie saves Ellen's life.

At the end of the novel, the war is over and Annemarie decides to wear Ellen's Star of David necklace, symbolizing her friendship with Ellen, until Ellen returns to claim it.

Lowry tells about the heroic acts of the Danes and portrays a deep friendship between Annemarie and Ellen that endures the oppression of the German soldiers to instill hope in readers for a world of human decency.

About the Characters

Annemarie Johansen

Annemarie is the protagonist, or main character in the novel, and can be seen as the heroine. She is a tall, blonde, ten-year-old Christian girl living in Copenhagen, Denmark during World War II. Annemarie is a dynamic character. She changes during the course of the novel due to her experiences and actions. We are aware of Annemarie's changes because Lowry narrates *Number the Stars* in the third person limited omniscient viewpoint in order to reveal Annemarie's thoughts and feelings.

When the novel begins, Annemarie is a relatively innocent child. She runs races with her best friend, Ellen Rosen, and plays paper dolls. She is annoyed because there are Nazi soldiers at every corner. She is aware of the changes that her family has had to adapt to, such as food and fuel shortages. Annemarie understands that she mustn't draw attention to herself, that she needs "to be one of the crowd." Everything has changed for Annemarie. The only constants in her life are fairy tales.

Annemarie begins to lose her innocence when she realizes that Ellen's life is in danger. She proves her friendship with Ellen many times by protecting her from the Nazis. At her house, she pulls Ellen's Star of David necklace off her neck to keep the Nazis from knowing that Ellen is Jewish. She later realizes that she must lie to protect Ellen and other Jews, so she pretends that she is mourning a great-aunt that doesn't exist. Finally, Annemarie faces the Nazis alone in the woods, and, relying on the Little Red Riding Hood fairy tale for courage, she bravely stands up to the Nazis.

Annemarie learns the meaning of bravery. She understands from her experience that ordinary people are called upon to be courageous. She also realizes that it is much easier to be courageous if you don't know the extent of the danger. Annemarie knows that bravery is the result of standing up for what you believe in, regardless of the dangers.

At the end of the novel, the war is over and Annemarie is hopeful that Ellen and her parents will return. As a symbol of her friendship with Ellen, she puts on Ellen's Star of David Necklace to wear until she can personally return it to Ellen.

Ellen Rosen

Ellen Rosen is a short, stocky, dark-haired, ten-year-old Jewish girl. She lives in Copenhagen, Denmark with her parents in the apartment above Annemarie's apartment. Ellen is Annemarie's best friend. Although we do not know Ellen's thoughts and feelings, we do know from Annemarie's observations that Ellen did change during the course of the novel.

Ellen is terrified when she is separated from her parents. She stays with the Johansens and when the Nazis come to the door demanding to know who she is, she courageously pretends to be Lise, Annemarie's older sister who is dead. Ellen goes with Annemarie, Kirsti, and Mrs. Johansen to Uncle Henrik's where she is soon reunited with her parents. At her parents side, "it was as if Ellen had moved . . . into a different world, the world of her own family and whatever lay ahead for them."

Ellen and her parents make it safely to neutral Sweden. After the war, Lowry does not reveal whether they return to Copenhagen, however the tone is hopeful that they will return.

Mr. and Mrs. Johansen and Henrik

Mr. and Mrs. Johansen are Annemarie's parents, and Henrik is her uncle. Mr. and Mrs. Johansen and Henrik are loving and wise people who have a positive influence on Annemarie. Mr. and Mrs. Johansen exhibit their bravery by protecting Ellen from the Nazis when the Nazis search their apartment, again on the train when the Nazis question their destination, and later at Uncle Henrik's house when the Jews are "paying their final respects" to Great-aunt Birte.

Uncle Henrik is also courageous. He is a fisherman. He risks his life, hiding Jews in the hollowed out area in the bottom of his boat, by taking them to neutral Sweden. All three people know what it means to be brave and to stand up for what you believe is right.

Peter Neilsen

Peter Neilsen was a redheaded young Danish man who had been engaged to Annemarie's sister, Lise. Peter had been like an older fun-loving brother to Annemarie and her sister, but after Lise's death, he changed. He rarely stopped by their apartment to visit, and when he did, he was rushed and serious. Sometimes he brought Annemarie's parents the *De Frie Danske*, an illegal newspaper backed by the Danish Resistance. The Danish Resistance was a group of courageous young people who secretly organized operations to bring harm to the Nazis and lead the Jewish people to safety.

Peter was instrumental in organizing the plan to help the Rosen family and the other Jews escape Nazi-occupied Denmark. While Ellen spent the night at the Johansens, Mr. and Mrs. Rosen were in hiding with Peter.

At the end of the novel, we learn that Peter was captured by the Germans and executed in the public square in Copenhagen. Peter died for what he believed—"he was proud to have done what he could for his country and for the sake of all free people."

Activities for Readers

1. The Star of David is an important symbol to the Jewish people. Research the significance of this symbol. Identify symbols important to other groups of people and discuss the significance of each.

2. Choose a scene from *Number the Stars* in which the Nazis' presence threatened the safety of Ellen and/or her family. Write the scene from Ellen's point of view.

3. Compare the escape route the Danish Resistance used to the Underground Railroad in the United States. Include information about the codes that were used to ensure the safety of the people escaping.

4. Using the Internet, locate information about the history of Denmark, as well as Denmark today. Find out whether landmarks cited by Lowry in the novel actually existed and whether they exist today.

Additional Resources

Chaston, Joel D. *Lois Lowry*. New York: Twayne Publishers, 1997.

Children's Literature Review. Vol. 46. Detroit: Gale Research, 1998: 25+.

Contemporary Authors New Revision Series. Vol. 13. Detroit: Gale Research, 1984: 333–336.

Contemporary Authors New Revision Series. Vol. 43. Detroit: Gale Research, 1994: 280–282.

Dinuzzo, Toni, et.al. "Learning About Lois Lowry." *Young Adult Literature.* Online. www.scils.rutgers.edu/special/kay/lowry.html.

Donahue, Rosanne. "Number the Stars." *Beacham's Guide to Literature for Young Adults.* Vol. 4. Washington, D.C.: Beacham Publishing, Inc., 1990: 1878–1882.

Haley-James, Shirley. "Lois Lowry." *The Horn Book Magazine.* August, 1990: 422–424.

Hurst, Carol. "Featured Author: Lois Lowry." Children's Literature Newsletter. Internet. www.carolhurst.com/authors/llowry.html.

Lowry, Lois. "Newbery Medal Acceptance." *The Horn Book Magazine.* August 1990: 412–421.

"Lois Lowry." Internet Public Library. Online. www.ipl.org/youth/AskAuthor/Lowry.html.

"Lois Lowry." Mountain Brook City Schools. Online. www.mtnbrook.k12.al.us/wf98/llowry2.htm.

Lorraine, Walter. "Lois Lowry." *The Horn Book Magazine.* July–August 1994: 423.

NEWBERY MEDAL WINNERS

Complete List of Newbery Medal Winners

2000: *Bud, Not Buddy* by Christopher Paul Curtis

1999: *Holes* by Louis Sachar

1998: *Out of the Dust* by Karen Hesse

1997: *The View From Saturday* by E.L. Konigsburg

1996: *The Midwife's Apprentice* by Karen Cushman

1995: *Walk Two Moons* by Sharon Creech

1994: *The Giver* by Lois Lowry

1993: *Missing May* by Cynthia Rylant

1992: *Shiloh* by Phyllis Reynolds Naylor

1991: *Maniac Magee* by Jerry Spinelli

1990: *Number the Stars* by Lois Lowry

1989: *Joyful Noise: Poems for Two Voices* by Paul Fleischman

1988: *Lincoln: A Photobiography* by Russell Freedman

1987: *The Whipping Boy* by Sid Fleischman

1986: *Sarah, Plain and Tall* by Patricia MacLachlan

1985: *The Hero and the Crown* by Robin McKinley

1984: *Dear Mr. Henshaw* by Beverly Cleary

1983: *Dicey's Song* by Cynthia Voigt

1982: *A Visit to William Blake's Inn: Poems for Innocent and Experienced Travelers* by Nancy Willard

1981: *Jacob Have I Loved* by Katherine Paterson

1980: *A Gathering of Days: New England Girl's Journal, 1830–1832* by Joan W. Blos

1979: *The Westing Game* by Ellen Raskin

1978: *Bridge to Terabithia* by Katherine Paterson

1977: *Roll of Thunder, Hear My Cry* by Mildred D. Taylor

1976: *The Grey King* by Susan Cooper

1975: *M.C. Higgins, the Great* by Virginia Hamilton

1974: *The Slave Dancer* by Paula Fox

1973: *Julie of the Wolves* by Jean Craighead George

1972: *Mrs. Frisby and the Rats of NIMH* by Robert C. O'Brien

1971: *Summer of the Swans* by Betsy Byars

1970: *Sounder* by William H. Armstrong

1969: *The High King* by Lloyd Alexander

1968: *From the Mixed-Up Files of Mrs. Basil E. Frankweiler* by E.L. Konigsburg

1967: *Up a Road Slowly* by Irene Hunt

1966: *I, Juan de Pareja* by Elizabeth Borton de Trevino

1965: *Shadow of a Bull* by Maia Wojciechowska

1964: *It's Like This, Cat* by Emily Neville

1963: *A Wrinkle in Time* by Madeleine L'Engle

1962: *The Bronze Bow* by Elizabeth George Speare

1961: *Island of the Blue Dolphins* by Scott O'Dell

1960: *Onion John* by John Krumgold

1959: *The Witch of Blackbird Pond* by Elizabeth George Speare

1958: *Rifles for Watie* by Harold Keith

1957: *Miracles on Maple Hill* by Virginia Sorensen

1956: *Carry On, Mr. Bowditch* by Jean Lee Latham

1955: *The Wheel on the School* by Meindert DeJong

1954: *. . . And Now Miguel* by John Krumgold

1953: *Secret of the Andes* by Ann Nolan Clark

1952: *Ginger Pye* by Eleanor Estes

1951: *Amos Fortune, Free Man* by Elizabeth Yates

1950: *The Door in the Wall* by Marguerite de Angeli

1949: *King of the Wind* by Marguerite Henry

1948: *The Twenty-One Balloons* by William Pène du Bois

1947: *Miss Hickory* by Carolyn Sherwin Bailey

1946: *Strawberry Girl* by Lois Lenski

1945: *Rabbit Hill* by Robert Lawson

1944: *Johnny Tremain* by Esther Forbes

1943: *Adam of the Road* by Elizabeth Janet Gray

1942: *The Matchlock Gun* by Walter Edmonds

1941: *Call It Courage* by Armstrong Sperry

1940: *Daniel Boone* by James Daugherty

1939: *Thimble Summer* by Elizabeth Enright

1938: *The White Stag* by Kate Seredy

1937: *Roller Skates* by Ruth Sawyer

1936: *Caddie Woodlawn* by Carol Ryrie Brink

1935: *Dobry* by Monica Shannon

1934: *Invincible Louisa: The Story of the Author of* Little Women by Cornelia Meigs

1933: *Young Fu of the Upper Yangtze* by Elizabeth Lewis

1932: *Waterless Mountain* by Laura Adams Armer

1931: *The Cat Who Went to Heaven* by Elizabeth Coatsworth

1930: *Hitty, Her First Hundred Years* by Rachel Field

1929: *The Trumpeter of Krakow* by Eric P. Kelly

1928: *Gay Neck, the Story of a Pigeon* by Dhan Gopal Mukerji

1927: *Smoky, the Cow Horse* by Will James

1926: *Shen of the Sea* by Arthur Bowie Chrisman

1925: *Tales from Silver Lands* by Charles Finger

1924: *The Dark Frigate* by Charles Hawes

1923: *The Voyages of Dr. Dolittle* by Hugh Lofting

1922: *The Story of Mankind* by Hendrik Willem van Loon

Index

NOTES

NOTES

NOTES

NOTES

NOTES

NOTES

NOTES

NOTES

CliffsNotes

LITERATURE NOTES

CliffsNotes™

@ cliffsnotes.com

Check Out the All-New CliffsNotes Guides

TECHNOLOGY TOPICS

PERSONAL FINANCE TOPICS

CAREER TOPICS